Being Middle Class in China

Many studies of the Chinese middle class focus on defining it and viewing its significance for economic development and its potential for sociopolitical modernisation. This book goes beyond such objective approaches and considers middle class people's subjective understanding and diverse experiences of class. Based on extensive original research including social surveys and detailed interviews, the book explores who the middle class think they are, what they think about a wide range of socioeconomic and sociopolitical issues, and why they think as they do. It examines attitudes towards the welfare state, social inequality, nationalism, relations with foreign countries and opinions on many social controversies, thereby portraying middle class people as more than simply luxury consumers and potential agents of democracy. The book concludes that a clear class identity and political consciousness have yet to emerge, but that middle class attitudes are best characterised as searching for a balance between old and new, the traditional and the foreign, the principled and the pragmatic.

Ying Miao is a Lecturer in China Studies at Xi'an Jiaotong-Liverpool University, China.

Routledge Studies on the Chinese Economy

Series Editor
Peter Nolan
Director, Centre of Development Studies;
Chong Hua Professor in Chinese Development; and
Director of the Chinese Executive Leadership Programme (CELP),
University of Cambridge

Founding Series Editors
Peter Nolan
University of Cambridge and
Dong Fureng
Beijing University

The aim of this series is to publish original, high-quality, research-level work by both new and established scholars in the West and the East, on all aspects of the Chinese economy, including studies of business and economic history.

For a complete list of titles in this series, please visit www.routledge.com/Routledge-Studies-on-the-Chinese-Economy/book-series/SE0706.

56 China's Centralized Industrial Order
Industrial reform and the rise of centrally controlled big business
Chen Li

57 China's Exchange Rate Regime
China Development Research Foundation

58 China's WTO Accession Reassessed
China Development Research Foundation

59 US-China Relations in the Twenty-First Century
A question of trust
Michael Tai

60 Understanding China
The Silk Road and the Communist Manifesto
Peter Nolan

61 Being Middle Class in China
Identity, attitudes and behaviour
Ying Miao

Being Middle Class in China

Identity, attitudes and behaviour

Ying Miao

First published 2017
by Routledge
2 Park Square, Milton Park, Abingdon, Oxon OX14 4RN

and by Routledge
711 Third Avenue, New York, NY 10017

Routledge is an imprint of the Taylor & Francis Group, an informa business

© 2017 Ying Miao

The right of Ying Miao to be identified as author of this work has been asserted by her in accordance with sections 77 and 78 of the Copyright, Designs and Patents Act 1988.

All rights reserved. No part of this book may be reprinted or reproduced or utilised in any form or by any electronic, mechanical, or other means, now known or hereafter invented, including photocopying and recording, or in any information storage or retrieval system, without permission in writing from the publishers.

Trademark notice: Product or corporate names may be trademarks or registered trademarks, and are used only for identification and explanation without intent to infringe.

British Library Cataloguing in Publication Data
A catalogue record for this book is available from the British Library.

Library of Congress Cataloging in Publication Data
A catalog record for this book has been requested.

ISBN: 978-1-138-18768-9 (hbk)
ISBN: 978-1-315-64301-4 (ebk)

Typeset in Times New Roman
by codeMantra

Contents

List of figures vii
List of tables ix
Acknowledgements xi
An illustrated glimpse into middle class life in Ningbo xii

Introduction 1

1 Class analysis in comparative perspective 7
Middle class Ningbo 9

2 Social identity of the middle class 12
Subjective interpretation of class terminologies 14
Middle strata, salaried class? 15
Relative deprivation and anxieties of the 'salaried class' 18
Beyond economic status: the subjective middle class 21
Economic security and cultural superiority:
  the imagined 'middle class' 26
Middle class identity and subjectivity 29

3 Between the state and the market 31
Personal income tax: 'honest worker's burden' 32
Health care: 'Sharp class conflict' 35
Education: 'Values over profit' 40
Pension: 'Neither here nor there' 43
Role of the state: 'Freedom within a safety net' 45
Negotiating the state and the market 48

4 Middle class attitude towards sociopolitical affairs 50
Social justice 51
Attitude towards democratic concepts 57

Case study: Food safety concerns 59
Case study: Zhenhai PX incident 63
Middle class and social stability 67
Understanding the paternalistic state 73

5 Nationalism among the middle class   77
Endogenous conceptions of being 'Chinese' 78
Chinese values versus universal values 79
Romanticising the past 82
Exogenous conception of the 'other' 86
The Chinese *middle class 97*

6 Viewing those below: the marginalised social groups   101
Gender 101
On homosexuality 104
On migrant workers 107
On children's education 112
The Yin and Yang of the Chinese middle class 117

Conclusion: the middle class in the Middle Kingdom   120
The 'Chinese', the 'middle' or the 'class'? 128
Imagining the Chinese middle class 131

Appendix   135
1. Normalised index and threshold for determining which factors are relatively significant 135
2. Threshold for determining significant correlation 135
Bibliography   137
Index   145

Figures

0.1	Luxury car and marriage	xii
0.2	Migrant worker in front of Häagen-Dazs	xiii
0.3	Nuclear family choosing imported food	xiv
0.4	Local food market	xv
0.5	Products targeted at the middle class	xvi
0.6	Advertising for school district housing	xvii
0.7	Popular streetside restaurants	xviii
2.1	Average spending when eating out	23
4.1	Main causal factors behind social inequality and injustice	52
4.2	Usage of 'equality' and 'equity' over time	55
4.3	In your opinion, how safe is the food in Ningbo?	59
5.1	Attitude towards foreign countries	86
6.1	Should migrant workers enjoy the same rights and treatment as urban residents in Ningbo?	108

Tables

1.1	Objective criteria for middle class status or membership	10
1.2	Middle class characteristics among the sampled respondents	10
2.1	Self-identified class category	16
2.2	How subjective class identities affect respondents' perception of class identity as a whole	17
2.3	Subjective assessment of standards of living: overall	19
2.4	Subjective assessment of standards of living: breakdown	19
2.5	Which shopping venues do you frequent?	23
3.1	How do you view the current personal income tax in China?	32
3.2	In your opinion, ownership of the healthcare system should be…	36
3.3	On a scale of 1 (save everything) to 10 (spend everything), how would you categorise your spending habits?	45
4.1	Fairness in society	51
4.2	Should there be income disparity in society?	51
4.3	Middle class attitudes towards democratic concepts	58
4.4	Attitude towards food safety	61
4.5	Involvement in PX incident	65
5.1	Attitude towards Chinese nationalism	79
5.2	Choose the closest statement that describes your attitude towards the Diaoyu Islands conflict	89
6.1	Choose the closest statement that describes your attitude towards 'leftover women'	102
6.2	Attitude towards children's education	113

Acknowledgements

This book could not have come into existence without the continuing support, unreserved encouragement and expert criticisms offered by a number of people. Professor Peter Nolan, who oversaw the meandering and often struggling process of transforming an idea and a question into a project and a book; whose words, actions and no nonsense advice not only taught me how to conduct research but also taught me how to be an academic. Professor David Goodman, whose unending patience, good humour and superhuman time management skills were instrumental in enabling the transition of this project from a thesis to a book, and transitioning myself from a PhD student to a starting lecturer and an early career researcher. I am especially thankful for his meticulous reading and editing of the manuscript on various occasions, hence, all mistakes that remain are mine. My gratitude goes to the following: numerous friends and esteemed colleagues in both the Centre of Development Studies, University of Cambridge, and the Department of China Studies, Xi'an Jiaotong-Liverpool University, who made the often idiosyncratic experience of academic pursuit enjoyable and rewarding; my parents, Ning Wang and Jiegang Miao, who are middle class maybe two days a week but scholarly curious and supportive always, who made everything possible; and finally, Dr. Yu Jia, my life partner and comrade in the scientific side of academia, who, despite preferring relativity to reflectivity, has been a constant source of comfort and cheer.

An illustrated glimpse into middle class life in Ningbo

Figure 0.1 **Luxury car and marriage**. Two cars on display beneath the offices buildings in the business district of Yinzhou, Ningbo. The billboard behind advertises a special promotion on 20th May, which phonetically sounds like 'I love you' in Mandarin, hence has been commercially dubbed as one of the Chinese valentine's days. The slogan '[Lower] price for you on 20th May' is a play on words for 'Marry you on 20th May' as 'price' and 'marry' is pronounced the same in Mandarin. Having fixed assets such as a car and a house is crucial to middle class identity in China, and interwoven with the idea of love and marriage, as there is high anxiety among the middle class that if they are unable to afford such 'big expenses', they are not fit for starting a family.

An illustrated glimpse into middle class life in Ningbo xiii

Figure 0.2 **Migrant worker in front of Häagen-Dazs**. A migrant worker walks by with a shoulder pole full of fruit in front of Häagen-Dazs. According to Ningbo Statistics Bureau, 43% of total population in Ningbo are migrants, making Ningbo the largest migrant-receiving city in Zhejiang province. The disparity in living standards among migrant workers and those with comfortable urban incomes are stark.

xiv *An illustrated glimpse into middle class life in Ningbo*

Figure 0.3 **Nuclear family choosing imported food**. A family peruses the imported milk and cheese section in the supermarket. After the Sanlu milk scandal of 2008, foreign imported milk jumped in sales, and food items such as cheese and butter not traditionally consumed in a Chinese diet have been increasingly popular among the middle class.

An illustrated glimpse into middle class life in Ningbo xv

Figure 0.4 **Local food market**. A shopper bargains with a seller at the local food market. Despite having typically lower prices and fresher produce, some middle class members avoid the local food markets as they believe the haggling and the self-picking required are not a good use of their time.

xvi *An illustrated glimpse into middle class life in Ningbo*

Figure 0.5 **Products targeted at the middle class**. Central display at Wanda Plaza, a popular shopping centre in Ningbo. Among the products promoted are massage chairs, suitcases and hoverboards, all geared towards the ideal middle class lifestyle of comfort and luxurious living.

An illustrated glimpse into middle class life in Ningbo xvii

Figure 0.6 **Advertising for school district housing.** A group of young parents standing in front of a stall advertising a new piece of residential real estate development boasting its prime location within a premium school district. The picture of the Big Ben and a young child with a school pack on the ad display, coupled with the words 'better education at earlier age' conjure images of a successful education culminating in studying abroad at prestigious universities. Such imagery symbolises the middle class dream of China, but also helps to bring a great deal of middle class anxiety not only because competition is intense, but the ingredients to success such as school district housing is often prohibitively expensive.

xviii   *An illustrated glimpse into middle class life in Ningbo*

Figure 0.7 **Popular streetside restaurants**. Popular streetside restaurants frequented by a range of patrons from white collar professionals to migrant workers. While hygiene and food safety are big concerns (garbage overflow on the streets, food not prepared according to safety standards and utensils are often not washed thoroughly), these streetside restaurants remain popular as they are quick, tasty, offer good value and sometimes become the social hub in the community.

Introduction

In August 2015, I was invited to stay in Aunt Lin's newly purchased summer retreat in central China. As we drove through the impressive gates and past the vast golf course designed exclusively for the residents, she recounted a tale of how she fended off a girl who wanted to marry into their household, but demanded too much financially. After she listed all the things the girl wanted, the summer villa among them, Aunt Lin exclaimed: 'Who does she think we are? We are but a middle class family, we are not rich'. A thoughtful pause later, she amended: 'Actually, we are just salaried class. A slightly better off salaried class family than others, but still! We work for our money, and money doesn't fall out of trees'.

Later, as I sat in Aunt Lin's open plan kitchen and living room with its own bar and home cinema, I asked her about the residential makeup of this high-end gated community. 'All middle class people, of course', was the unsurprising answer. 'We earn our money, and want a place to retreat privately, away from prying eyes'. Mansions in this plot of land cost easily upwards of five million CNY (£500,000), over fifty times what is considered the annual salary of a middle class person in China (around 90,000 CNY). Yet, for Aunt Lin, she was 'salaried class' when talking about her wealth, and becomes 'middle class' only when taking pride in her cultured conduct and class tastes.

It's hard to say whether Aunt Lin can be described as 'typical' Chinese middle class. On the one hand, business analysts who claim the Chinese middle class are vanguard consumers will no doubt recognise her capacity and willingness to consume luxury products (Barton, Chen and Jin 2013). She is also educated, reasonably well-informed and certainly opinionated about politics and current affairs, with an affinity for the foreign, the modern, and some might say, the liberal and the universal (Wasserstrom 2008; Fukuyama 2013). On the other hand, she works for the state, has a keen vested interest in the state, and despite her grumblings, would never dream of going against the state (Tomba 2009; Tang 2011). Whatever characteristics that has been ascribed to the so-called Chinese middle class, from most perspectives, she can fit the bill.

A few weeks later, I interviewed Joyce, a 27-year-old lawyer. She also considered herself middle class: an elite education in one of the best universities in Beijing, a job working for a large corporate firm that puts her overall earnings just above the middle class income line. In her undergraduate years, she would exchange notes with her classmates on which professor had the most interesting 'avant-garde' views on politics, and claimed these lectures 'opened her mind'. Like her peers in the legal profession, she believes in democracy and the rule of law (Michelson and Liu 2010), and like many others I have interviewed, she sees the logic in the current status quo and does not challenge it. What is more interesting is that she does not recognise any class peers by virtue of shared profession or income, despite imagining a group of middle class peers somewhere who share her values and outlook in life.

Like Aunt Lin, Joyce can also fit the 'middle class' bill, but from a different perspective. Yet, there is a good chance that they do not recognise each other as class peers. Nor do they really share the same political outlook when you look closely: while neither of them would dream of challenging China's political status quo, they have identified different 'pressure points' in the system that should be reformed, that happens to be two competing interest groups. Same with their affinity for the so-called liberal views: for them, democracy mean different things, and comes at different prices. Again, depending on the observational angle, they are both similar in sharing the 'middle class' label assigned by conventional metrics, and distinct as they do not uniformly exhibit the so-called 'middle class' characteristics. How can these individuals, at once similar and different, come together in helping us understand China's rising urban affluent, the so-called emerging 'middle class'?

On the one hand, this question seems superfluous, as official rhetoric tells us that China is barrelling towards the Chinese dream of a 'middle class society'. On the other hand, there has always been considerable methodological challenges in pinpointing the so-called Chinese middle class. Not only is there still much debate on how to define the middle class, and whether a middle class in the sociological sense exists in China at all (Li 2009; Goodman 2012), even when a social category resembling 'middle class' has been defined and 'found', they appear to be politically ambiguous. Scholars argue over whether they are social stabilisers (Tomba 2009; Tang 2011) or proponents of reform (Li et al. 2008); or indeed whether they share a common value at all. Although there is now a consensus over the multiplicity of this social group (Li 2010b), attempts to understand its heterogeneity have largely been focused on identifying 'micro-classes' with distinct occupational and political features, especially with regard to their relationship with the state (Dickson 2010; Chen 2015; Lu 2016). Individuals like Aunt Lin and Joyce would no doubt be eligible for much of these studies, which arrive at seemingly different conclusions. Such discrepancy is evocative of an Asian proverb: that the study of the so-called Chinese middle class is akin to 'blind men groping an elephant'.

This book is not an attempt to further clarify who the elusive middle class are, or predict how they will impact China's sociopolitical future. Instead, this book is an attempt to look at a group of so-called middle class individuals *as they are*, without necessarily extrapolating what they *represent*. In fact, this book simply looks at the manifold meanings of being 'middle' in urban China – what it means to live a relatively affluent life, to have a good education and to be well informed, to work in a white-collar occupation, and how these circumstances shape people's attitudes, values and behaviour.

To achieve these objectives, this book explores a number of topics that are Here and elsewhere: seldom asked in the context of middle class studies in China. Indeed, there is more to be gained from the Chinese middle class than the typical portrayal of a luxury consumer who is either vocally demanding of his political rights, or afraid of upsetting the state in case it jeopardised his new found riches. One of the key deficiencies in existing research is that questions are seldom asked about the middle class outside of the context of its purchasing power and democratising role: few studies have been conducted on how they view themselves, how they view the outside world, and almost none on how they view a multitude of social issues that are perhaps not immediately political but nevertheless illuminating of their values and attitudes at large. While research on Chinese nationalism, Confucian values and social injustices in China are abundant on their own, they are almost never considered with the middle class in mind. It is as if on these topics the middle class automatically blends into the background and becomes indistinguishable from its peers, which seems to be more of an oversight than a reasonable assumption.

Furthermore, most research on the subject of middle class attitudes and behaviour focuses on finding out the 'what', rather than the 'why': this lies at the heart of the 'blind men and the elephant' fallacy. Without carefully unravelling the logic of thinking behind these attitudes and behaviour, the picture we observe is always incomplete, and contradictory and paradoxical findings are likely. To understand this complex and heterogeneous social group, we need to look beyond the 'who' and the 'what' and start asking the 'why'. Thus, this book also aims to explore the intricate relationship between, and complex thinking behind, middle class identity, attitudes and behaviour.

The research ethos of this book differs from its predecessors in the field in two ways. First, it is worth noting that even though the phrase 'Chinese middle class' is used throughout this book, the intention is not to equate the respondents described with the social group at large, or to generalise their behaviour and assume that the same characteristics may apply to their peers elsewhere. The logic is that they count as members of the so-called Chinese middle class, hence, we will refer to them as such. They are not, however, representative of the elusive 'middle class' in China as a whole. The reason for this kind of approach is to find out 1) whether it is possible to have people who fall under the middle class category by objective identification but do not fit the 'middle class profile', and 2) if yes, whether we can learn more about their attitudes and mindset by asking them more questions. Because of the non-representativeness of this study, a simple and widely used middle class categorisation was used, and some well-trodden survey topics had to be repeated just to better situate the sample of respondents against the national average. This mixed-methods approach both allows us to contextualise the middle class respondents in this book against their national peers, as well as set them apart by looking at them as 'persons', rather than numbers and aggregates.

Second, this study pays more attention to the layered reasoning behind the respondents' attitudes and behaviour, by asking them questions on a generic level, then introducing case studies based on real-life events, or implying scenarios that are more related to their everyday lives. This line of questioning serves to pinpoint the intricate space between what 'should be', what 'could be' and what 'is'. In doing so, certain results are found to be seemingly contradictory that are actually due to differences in assimilated and segregated thinking, which explains how and why the middle class might appear to agree to something in principle, but would not act upon such principles in real life.

Due to the specificity of the research goal, this study sought to gather a predominantly middle class sample for an intra-class analysis, rather than seek a representative sample across the population and conduct an inter-class comparison. Again, the point is to illustrate that the sampled respondents of this study could fit within the 'conventional' middle class category, yet they may not necessarily correspond to conventional middle class characteristics, or our understanding of it. Instead of observing middle class as a 'social class', this book aims to look at middle class as a 'social category', by paying more attention to the people who might fit under this categorical label, and are often quoted in global headlines, rather than the nature of the category itself. Adjustments were thus made in the methodology: survey questions were distributed in a digital, online form, not only because the anonymity encouraged people to participate but also because being connected to the Internet is a key indicator of being middle class. A snow-balling method was used to maximise response, so that the respondents were more likely to receive the survey through their social network (deemed more trustworthy) while allowing them to retain anonymity should they choose to participate. The objective class positions of these respondents were ascertained through three control criteria: income, occupation and education. The survey gathered a total of 439 participants from the fieldwork site in Ningbo, Zhejiang, and 19 respondents were drafted for in-depth interviews.

This book has six chapters. The first two chapters introduce the conceptualisation of the middle class and present the particular middle class sample in this book. Chapter three explores whether and to what extent the same group of individuals who might be categorised as 'middle class' by objective terms identifies with their class labels, to determine if the middle class *think* they are middle class at all. The results indicate a notable discrepancy between objective class positions and subjective class identity, as a sizeable proportion of the respondents categorised themselves as 'salaried class' (*gongxin jieceng,* 工薪阶层) instead of 'middle class'. This discrepancy is not simply due to an imprecise understanding of class terminology, as there is a difference in where they place themselves in the context of the social order, and where they place the imagined 'middle class', and what being middle class should mean. More often than not, these respondents chose to identify with a class label by first eliminating all the labels that they think do not apply to themselves, thus highlighting a key problem in the study of middle class as a social group: that the use of the same class label does not imply social cohesion. Thus, the objective middle class may be similar to each other in their economic reality, but are divided in their social identity, thus calling into question whether they are likely to share any similar outlooks, or will act upon their similarities. The self-identified labels of 'salaried class' and 'middle class' are also employed throughout the book to explore the extent to which subjective class identity has an impact on the respondents' attitudes and behaviours; thus, it should be noted that unless otherwise specified, they always refer to the respondents' subjective class labels as given in the control survey questions, rather than a reflection of any objective positions.

Chapter four examines middle class attitudes towards key public institutions, such as health care, education, and pension, and assesses whether the middle class prefer state ownership of these institutions or privatisation of these institutions. The findings illustrate how the middle class view the state, in terms of its socio-economic responsibilities: that the state is expected to provide 'safety net' features for the disadvantaged, as well as regulate the macro-environment in which individuals could operate, but it is not expected to cover the areas where individuals could control themselves. The key here is that the respondents demonstrated a high level of empathy for the limits of government, which is not held blindly accountable for every failing in the system. Thus, the pressure for reform in these areas is related to the amount of *effort* the government is expending, rather than the *regime* under which the government operates.

Similarly in chapter five, the middle class is shown to have a keen awareness of social injustice and a high level of democratic support, but exhibited little to no desire for change. Again, the drive for reform is offset by their understanding of the sociopolitical environment at large, the consensus that the state cannot be solely responsible for the inequalities and inequities in society, but it is the most viable and competent vessel for change. Due to their level of education and socio-economic position, which grant them a sound knowledge and experience of the state apparatus, the middle class is particularly adept at separating what 'should be', what 'could be' and what 'is'. The idea that they could recognise the merits of egalitarian and democratic reform in principle, but would not advise it, nor deem it likely, in day-to-day reality is at the centre of their seemingly contradictory attitudes and responses.

Chapter six deals with how the Chinese middle class view themselves in terms of their national identity, and how they view their neighbours and some of the world's superpowers. The findings indicate that the middle class is able to differentiate between culture and politics when assessing countries that have a political past with China (i.e. Japan and America), although the same level of reluctant respect is not afforded in other Third World nations, such as India, North Korea and the Philippines. Meanwhile, they are receptive to foreign ideas while remaining firmly rooted in their national identity, and they hold the belief that different value systems should be made compatible. Thus, it appears that the Chinese middle class are at once nationalistic and international, with a mind for the absorption and adaptation of different ideals, which is remarkably similar to how China has adapted to foreign influence over the years as a whole.

This process of finding an intermediate space between two opposing sides is highlighted again in chapter six, which examines middle class attitudes towards a variety of controversial social issues. Here the difference between public attitudes and private behaviour becomes even clearer: the respondents could readily accept the need for tolerant and accepting attitudes towards a range of social issues without having to subject their private lives to the same type of moral guidelines. Although appearing to be principled and liberal in their attitudes, again the middle class are very pragmatic about how these principles would translate into reality, they are aware of the potential difficulties involved and would seek to circumvent them by taking preventative action whenever possible, even if it means compromising in what they claim to believe in. Such pragmatism and compromise are illustrative of the middle class struggle to find a balance in a transitional society, where the individual is constantly coming into conflict with the larger environment.

The wide range of topics covered in this book allows a multi-angled view in a particular sample of the middle class in Ningbo. At first glance, they are just as fragmentary, disunited and contradictory as previous studies have portrayed. Upon closer inspection, however, there is a level of consistency behind their attitudes, behaviour and thinking. They appear paradoxical only if viewed through dichotomic lens; thus, it is inadequate to try to understand the Chinese middle class by placing them on either end of a binary scale. Indeed, by virtue of their 'middle-ness' they are constantly reacting to, and reflective of, their surroundings; the process of finding and maintaining a balance is paramount to their identity and survival. In search for the space between wealth and culture, the national and the international, democracy and stability, the public and the private, the collective and the individual, their seemingly conflictory attitude and behaviour are in fact a constant negotiation between what 'should be', what 'could be' and what 'is'. To understand the Chinese middle class, then, it is best to utilise a Chinese religious ideology, i.e. the Taoist idea of Yin and Yang embodied by a fish with its head to its tail. Unlike most of the Abrahamic religions that have bred a dualistic mode of thinking in the West (Nadeau 2013), the Taoist Yin Yang fish symbolises one of the key ideas still deeply influential in China today: the idea of a complementary, rather than opposing, relationship between two different factors. The two sides of Yin and Yang denote being and potentiality, they are reflective of, revolve around and depend on one another. There is no other social group quite like the middle class who can understand and employ this idea to its fullest. Well educated and newly affluent, they experience increased exposure to Western, universal and liberal ideas that may run counter to their national, collective and traditional beliefs. To navigate and keep up in the rapidly evolving environment, the middle class are constantly searching for the middle road that is true to their name. After all, society is changing and so are they; adhering to one set of labels and beliefs too strictly and disallowing pragmatic change indicate risking being cast aside by the tides of time. Thus, the Chinese middle class are at its core an accurate reflection of modern China as a nation: seeking the harmony of balance amid the shadows of chaos.

1 Class analysis in comparative perspective

For a long time, research on class and social stratification has been mostly concerned with two concepts: class structure, which includes class location and class relations; and class agency, which incorporates class interests, consciousness, formation, practices and struggle. Those who take the structuralist approach, from classical theorists like Marx and Weber to the more recent Nuffield researchers of Goldthorpe and Marshall, suggest that social relations are rooted in division of labour and employment relations, and recently, occupational locations (Marx 1845; Davis and Moore 1945; Goldthorpe *et al.* 1969; Marshall 1997; Wright 2005). On the other hand are those who focus on the intentionality, knowledgeability of the self-conscious agents and their ability to construct, negotiate or struggle against the social world they are in, usually in the form of class culture (Bourdieu 1984; Agger 1991; Skeggs 2004; Bennett *et al.* 2009; Paton 2014). As such, scholars often argued over the class structure/agency duality and its implications of class determinism versus class voluntarism. Gidden's structuration theory attempted to reconcile this dualism by arguing that structure and agency are intertwined (Giddens 1981), and indeed a substantial amount of research has illustrated how forms of collective actions can be sustained by drawing on class resources by agents (Lash and Urry 1987) and can be explained by the class capacities that allow them to pursue their interests (Savage 2005).

However, in the latter half of the twentieth century, the transition between industrial to financial capitalism in the Euro-American context has led to the increase of individualisation and the decline of working class culture, which have caused some to believe that class is no longer either relevant or able to produce taken-for-granted ways of behaviour, values and views (Beck 1992; Pakulski and Waters 1996; Beck 2002; Atkinson 2010). Nevertheless, inequalities in life chance, income, health persist, and economic inequalities continue to be implicated in wider social, cultural and political divisions. Rather than continuing to find new ways to define class in a precise and contained manner, researchers have paid increasing attention to processes of culture, lifestyle and taste, and argued that economic inequalities (arising out of market processes) and social inequalities (as a result of cultural and sociopolitical differences) need to be considered together. In particular, class processes can be seen as operational, as long as economic and cultural practices work together to reproduce inequality and hierarchy, regardless of whether people are conscious of class issues or receptive to class identities (Devine 1998; Devine and Savage 1999; Bottero 2004; Tyler 2015). Indeed, class is now seen as 'modes of differentiation rather than types of collectivity' (Savage 2000; Crompton 2006).

By comparison, research on social stratification in China has also experienced a decline in the 1980s, albeit due to different contextual reasons. Whereas class lost its ideological significance in the West due to new developments in modern industrial societies such as the advent of pluralism and individualisation, class lost its discursive legitimacy in China after the state consciously abandoned the idea of class struggle as it chose to adopt marketisation and partial privatisation. There followed a period where the idea of class was both rejected as a political tool as well as a social reality, and interest in the study of social stratification was renewed only as a result of the rapidly evolving and deepening inequalities brought on by the market reform. Among the factors shaping China's new socioeconomic contours are both distinct features belonging to China's market socialism, such as the household registration system (Huang, Guo and Tang 2010), the cadre versus professional dualism (Zang 2008), as well as familiar influences of consumption (Hanser 2008; Davis and Wang 2009) and individualisation (Halskov Hansen and Svarverud 2010) that also manifest the process and characteristics of China's social stratification in distinct forms.

From the beginning of the twenty-first century onwards, there has been increasing attention paid to the rise of the middle class in developing countries, China chiefly among them. Not only has the Chinese state continuously emphasised the importance of the middle class as a part of its expanding rhetoric regarding a 'well-off society' and the prosperous 'China Dream', Western commentators and business analysts alike have been eager to highlight the significance of the rising urban affluent populace, both in terms of its consumption power and its sociopolitical role. In pursuit of this middle class, scholars have encountered similar problems to the study of class in general in the Euro-American context: in terms of its definitional criteria, its characteristics and its wider political implication (Li 2010a). Some contest that the middle class are more of a rhetoric than a sociopolitical reality (Goodman 2012), or that there is no difference between the middle class or the 'middle stratum' (Li 2008c). Others point to the heterogeneity of the 'middle classes', how individuals in similar middle class occupations can have extremely different educational attainment levels and family backgrounds because of historical and political reasons (Zhu 1998; Li 2008a), and how the professionals, managers, cadres, even professors and lawyers all have the potential to exhibit distinct characteristics (Bian *et al.* 2005; Tang and Unger 2013; Wu and Zhang 2015). Nearly every researcher agrees that income is a problematic criterion for defining middle class, but there is little agreement over what is better or more feasible (Zhang 2008; Li 2010b). Like similar debates that have happened in the Western context, scholars and commentators alike argue over whether middle class are inherently conservative by virtue of their socioeconomic status and sociopolitical ties with the state (Tomba 2009; Lu 2010; Chen 2013; Goodman 2014b), or whether their education and contact with the outside world will lead them to demand greater political roles and even democratisation. Among the plethora of studies, the only fairly uncontested understanding about the Chinese middle class seems to be that the middle class have heterogeneous social compositions, have strong ties to the party-state, and cannot be simply defined by income alone. Although structure and agency both exist, they are also ambiguous. To paraphrase the words of E. P. Thompson, the middle class in China may very well be a 'happening'.

Thus, we come back to the question posed in the first chapter of this book. How can two individuals who do not recognise each other as class peers, despite having similar socioeconomic statuses and at times ascribe similar class labels to themselves, come together to shed light on this so-called Chinese middle class? The key is that despite the fragmentary and heterogeneous nature of their social composition and identities, there is a remarkable degree of continuity in their mode of differentiation, internalisation and exclusion of their class identities and experience. Sometimes the nuanced distinctions in their class experience affects their attitude as members of subjective classes, sometimes they come together and use similar logics of differentiation and exclusion that see them emerge as a more cohesive middle class. The way they continuously negotiate, balance and extrapolate the social world that they inhabit is both the result of their overall socioeconomic position and is illustrative of their daily experience of being middle in the 'Middle Kingdom'.

Middle class Ningbo

Located in the affluent southern coastal area of China, Ningbo was one of the first cities to open up under the Treaty of Nanking (1842), and have since remained an important port city in the region. According to the Ningbo Statistical Yearbook, the urban population of Ningbo in 2012 is just over 2.2 million, of whom 1.4 million are registered as non-agricultural. For the same year, the average annual disposable income per capita of urban residents is ¥38,043, while the average total expenditure for consumption per capita is ¥22,887. Comparatively, the average annual disposable income per capita among the 36 major cities in China, which is ¥27,319 in 2011, and the average total expenditure for consumption per capita among these major cities is ¥19,283. There are half a million private cars registered in the urban area of Ningbo alone, and approximately 1.3 million residents are connected to the Internet (Ningbo Statistics Bureau 2012). Among the 1.7 million residents who are employed, more than 30% have had higher education, and 15% have received an undergraduate degree or above. Famous for being home to many 'Confucian merchants' – merchants who have an affinity for learning and aspired to be the Confucian 'gentleman' in their conduct – and housing the Tianyi Pavillion, the oldest existing library in China, Ningbo is a city known for its entrepreneurial spirit and education. With a per capita output of gross domestic product (GDP) of ¥112,653, Ningbo counts among the 'booming middle class city' as outlined both in the state rhetoric and in commentator's eyes.

It was not difficult to find a sample of respondents in Ningbo who befit the objective middle class category. By limiting the survey to those with Internet connectivity, and distributing the survey among online communities and instant messaging groups of large private cooperate enterprise, a medium-sized real-estate firm, a medium-sized insurance firm, and a regional car owners club, the overwhelming majority of the respondents returned can be called middle class by at least one of the objective criteria (Li and Zhang 2008a).

Table 1.1 Objective criteria for middle class status or membership

		Survey part I (%) (n=181)	Survey part II (%) (n=258)
Income	>87.5 k (high income)	49 (89/181)	37 (96/258)
(¥ per annum)	60–87.5 k	14 (25/181)	20 (52/258)
	35–60 k	20 (37/181)	21 (54/258)
	<35 k (low income)	5 (9/181)	9 (22/258)
	N/A	12 (21/181)	13 (34/258)
Occupation	White collar	74	76
	Non-white collar	26	24
Education	Higher education	93	92
	No higher education	7	8

Table 1.2 Middle class characteristics among the sampled respondents

Statement	Percentage
Foreign exposure	
Percentage who spoke serviceable English (n=258)	30
Percentage who read foreign newspapers, such as *The New York Times* (n=258)	13
Percentage who watch foreign TV news, such as the CNN, Fox and the BBC (n=258)	21
Percentage who watch foreign TV shows and films on a regular basis (n=258)	73
Percentage who celebrate Western holidays, such as Christmas, Valentine's Day and Halloween (n=181)	65
Residential standards	
Percentage who own private cars (n=181)	63
Percentage who have art or paintings in their home (n=181)	37
Percentage who live in commercial housing districts, brownstone districts or villas	78
Consumption habits	
Percentage who prefer green/organic food (n=258)	63
Percentage who prefer imported foods over domestic when funds permit (n=258)	71
Percentage who shop in high-end malls (n=181)	25
Percentage whose durable goods are usually luxury brands (n=181)	23
Percentage who travel for leisure at least once a year (n=258)	78

Among these respondents, 32 per cent were state employees, 46 per cent were men, and 31 per cent were Chinese Communist Party (CCP) members. Other questions posed in the surveys give additional insight into this particular sample of the respondents' 'middle class-ness': the majority of them live in high-quality commercial housing districts or above, own private cars and travel for leisure at least once a year. They are fairly exposed to foreign influences and consume foreign media, many celebrate foreign holidays and a third speak serviceable English. Despite a relatively modest percentage who engage in luxury shopping, there is a fairly high percentage of people who prefer green/organic food and imported food, consistent with the avant-garde nature of the middle class populace in other countries.

It is hard to say whether this sample of affluent, well-educated respondents are representative of the Chinese middle class. What is certain is that they exhibit many characteristics that have been ascribed as typical to the middle class, so that they cannot be discounted. Indeed, some of the findings in later chapters show that they exhibit similar attitudes in certain areas concordant with other middle class studies in China, and by virtue of objective criteria such as income, they have been referred to as 'middle class' in headlines domestic and foreign alike. Among these surveyed respondents who grant us an overall picture of their attitudes and behaviour, 19 respondents who satisfied all three objective middle class criteria (income, education and white collar occupation) were drafted into in-depth interviews, and they in turn give us additional insight into how they manage their sociopolitical identities and expectations in China's evolving socioeconomic landscape. Together the survey and interviews offer us a window into what being middle class, or middle stratum, means in China.

2 Social identity of the middle class

Although the social sciences generally saw the 'death of class' debate in the last few decades (Beck 1992), there has been a revival in class analysis moving away from the focus on rigid class categories based on occupation, to a more flexible, encompassing look at class identity and culture as both the product and reproduction of social inequality (Crompton and Scott 1999; Devine and Savage 1999; Savage 2003; Tyler 2015). This shift, however, has predominantly been occurring in examination of the Euro-American context. In the context of developing countries such as China, relatively little attention has been paid to the people's subjective understanding and experience of class in China (Li 2010b, 2013). Yet, a degree of consensus remains in social science in general that class labels are still being utilised at an individual level, especially in relational terms (Savage 2003; Bottero 2004; Skeggs 2015). After all, without a subjective sense of belonging, any objective social category can only remain a category, and not a true 'social group' with class consciousness (Thompson 1963).

Indeed, one of the key obstacles in ascribing a consistent sociopolitical function to the Chinese middle class is that they are far from being a homogeneous group (Goodman and Chen 2013). While income, white collar occupation and higher education provide a relatively straightforward and popular way of categorising the middle class in China, research has already shown that such 'external individualistic factors' are often inconsistent, or less crucially relevant, to the emergence of class identity (Liu 2001; Zhao 2004b). Family background and marital status (Zhen 2001; Li 2010b), geographical location and mobility (You and Xu 2007), age and Communist Party membership (Hou 2010), as well as the respondents' sense of relative deprivation and ideological persistence (Guo 2001; Lu 2002), have all been found to have a significant impact on subjective class identities. Within the broadly defined middle class, distinctive class characteristics and attitudes can be found between professionals, managerial personnel and officials; specific social groups such as lawyers and students; or more importantly, between those who have different positions in, and relationships with, the party-state (Yi 2008; Li 2010a). Due to the vastly fragmented and overwhelming heterogeneity of this newly affluent social category, some scholars have argued that there is in fact no (meaningful) middle class in China at all (Li 2008c; Goodman 2014b).

Nevertheless, the fact remains that with the official discourse on *xiaokang* society [literally: 'a healthy (well-off) society'] and middle class society, the idea of being middle class is now deeply rooted in Chinese minds. National surveys have consistently shown that a large proportion of the Chinese population consider themselves as middle class: the World Value Survey in 2012 reports 43.9 per cent middle class respondents in its national representative sample, consistent with Li Chunling's 2008 study, while Zhou Xiaohong's urban study reports a middle class proportion as high as 85.5 per cent (Zhou 2008). Meanwhile, estimates for objective middle class categorisations fluctuate between 3.1 per cent and 25 per cent (Li 2010b). Not only do the numbers among studies not match but notable discrepancies have been found between the objective economic realities and the subjective class identities of the same survey samples, both in terms of self-overestimation and self-underestimation (Li 2005; Li and Zhang 2008b). These findings illustrate one of the key problems in the study of the Chinese middle class: the fact that being labelled middle class by objective indicators does not necessarily reflect a subjective sense of belonging, either with the class label itself, or with their class peers; nor do the beliefs of belonging to the middle class necessarily reflect their economic reality. There is a clear mismatch between not only class categorisation and class identity, but also between class position and class experience.

In this chapter, it emerges that only half of the respondents who befit the objective middle class category had consistent self-ascribed middle class identities, despite the fact that nearly two-thirds of them positioned themselves around the middle of society. Instead, there is a popular use of a 'salaried class' label by a significant portion of the objective middle class that is overlooked by academia. This set of 'salaried class' identities, literally translated as 'stratum of [those earning] working salaries' (*gongxin jieceng*, 工薪阶层), is far removed from the historical and political connotations of 'working class' (*gongren jieceng*, 工人阶层); instead, it rests on the members' belief that their lack of supplementary income outside of their 'working salary' separates them from the true 'middle class', who are able to afford an anxiety-free lifestyle due to their financial stability. This type of belief has led them to look towards economic indicators as the primary determinants of class, whereas those who are consistent in their middle class identities and positions typically place a heavier emphasis on the cultural indicators of class, arguing that it is the initiative of adopting a cultured and mannered lifestyle that separates them from members of other classes.

In constructing their respective class identities, both groups use similar imaginings of the ideal 'middle class', whose cultured lifestyle rests upon strong economic foundations. However, the income prerequisites for the 'imagined middle class' often differ greatly from the scholarly definition, and the 'soft', cultural indicators are often too subjective and imprecise to fit within a clear objective framework. Thus, the point of contrast is usually made through a definition by exclusion, rather than inclusion, suggesting that in the Chinese context, too, people are more confident of class differences than similarities (for research on negative labels of class in Western contexts, see Sennett 1972; Coyner 1977; Ehrenreich 1989). This observation whereby people are more aware of class differences than similarities highlights another problem whereby the study of the middle class in developing countries, when approaching class as an analytical tool of socioeconomic origin and with sociopolitical consequence, assumes class cohesion based on social categorisation and identification, instead of a collective identity that does not necessarily rely upon its scholarly definition, and can be built mainly upon social comparison. Indeed, if the middle class were to develop certain patterns of behaviour and attitudes according to their class definitions, it would be because of who *they* think they are, not who the *observers* think they are. In the case of this study, it is clear that the objective middle class group found in Ningbo have no coherent subjective middle class identity; moreover, their imagined 'ideal' middle class individual is someone whose financial stability and cultural superiority in personal life would inspire overall stability in society, thus unlikely to play the part of the political advocate.

Subjective interpretation of class terminologies

The use of class terminologies in China, due to their historical background, is often vague and imprecise. The political rhetoric of class in the Mao era, which is well within living memory, was such that class comprised of three key elements: *jieji* (class); *chengfen*; (social role) and *chushen* (social origin); and that society was de-stratified and comprised of only two classes (workers and peasants) and one intermediate stratum of intellectuals (Guo 2012). Nevertheless, subsequent researchers have shown that even then (or perhaps more so then), the sociological reality of China's social stratification was vastly different from the official discourse (Whyte 1985; Bian 2002), and that the disjuncture was well understood popularly.

After the reform era began, class terminologies lost their political ramifications, and instead took on new popular meanings, evolving through media and the Internet. Whereas sociological research saw the distinction between working class and middle class as primarily occupational (blue collar versus white collar), in popular perception this distinction appears not to be the case – in *Baidu Baike*, China's own version of Wikipedia, 'working class' is defined as 'those who earn a working salary, and do not own their own company', a claim that appears to be unsubstantiated by any academic sources. Compared to the even more anachronistic term of '*gongren jieji*' (literally: class of workers), the literal interpretation of *gongxin jieceng* as 'stratum of [those earning] working salaries' bears more resemblance to the so-called 'salaryman', a term that originated from Japan but has increasingly gained popularity in the West, to denote white collar workers. Thus, the idea of the working class in China has virtually lost all of its proletariat connotations, particularly in the revolutionary sense. Instead, a distinction is drawn between those whose income comprises solely, or mainly, their working salary, and those whose incomes are supplemented by other means of financial returns, such as from the stock market and real estate investment.

The absolute *sum* of one's income did not matter as much as the *type* of income one had:

> To me, no matter if you earn ¥5000 a month or ¥50,000 a month, as long as you earn a working salary, you are salaried class.
> —*Kun*

The expression 'middle class/middle strata' is literally translated as 'class of middle property', with the key element being the character 产 (*chan*). Consequently, income and other externally identifiable indicators of wealth were seen as the foundations of the middle social category, as expressed below:

> The importance [in middle class] is the word *chan* (property). Without property and material wealth, you can't count someone as middle class.
> —*Wang*

It is worth noting that although many surveys, including the one conducted here, use the term 'middle strata' without the emphasis on property, it is still referred to and understood as the middle class. Indeed, the data show that economic indicators are the most significant factors in the respondents' internalisation of their class, middle or otherwise. This shows that economic well-being still underlines perceived class positions, in that it provides a solid foundation for their class identity.

Middle strata, salaried class?

There are two usual ways to ascertain an individual's subjective position in society: by asking him to grade himself on a linear social spectrum, or by asking him to place himself in a given class category. The one who positioned himself in the middle of society, or into the middle class category, is usually considered as self-identified middle class. The former approach offers more flexibility by removing potentially murky connotations of class from social stratification itself, while the latter provides a more concrete setting for subjective class identification. However, even with the latter categorisation, class is typically given interchangeably with 'strata', and denotes one's identification of position in society rather than any identification with a label with sociological meaning. For instance, 'working class' is usually not included in the categories given, despite its lasting significance in academic research, as well as its widespread usage in public. When the term '*gongxin jieceng*' is included alongside other conventional class categories in a survey in Ningbo, an interesting mismatch appeared: in a sample of 181 middle class respondents by objective criteria, 66 per cent placed themselves around the middle of society (four to six on the social spectrum), 79 per cent middle and above (four and above), but only 46 per cent considered themselves specifically 'middle class', while 48 per cent considered themselves 'salaried class' instead (Table 2.1). This specific mismatch is not affected by their perceived position in

Table 2.1 Self-identified class category

Subjective class identity		% of total respondents	% of respondents who believe they belong to the middle strata (4–6 on the social spectrum)	% of respondents who satisfy the 'high income' criteria
Middle class	Upper middle class	4 (9/181)	4 (5/120)	8 (7/89)
	Middle class	24 (45/181)	24 (29/120)	37 (33/89)
	Lower middle class	16 (30/181)	21 (25/120)	18 (16/89)
	Total	46 (84/181)	49 (59/120)	63 (56/89)
Salaried class		48 (87/181)	48 (58/120)	35 (37/89)
Other		5 (10/181)	3 (3/120)	2 (2/89)

society (only 49 per cent of those who placed themselves in the middle of society saw themselves as middle class), nor income (35 per cent of those who satisfied the high-income criteria still considered themselves as salaried class).

Furthermore, it is found that as their subjective class identities differ, so did their emphasis on class markers, both of their own, and of others (Table 2.2).

Table 2.2 shows that the salaried class respondents are primarily concerned with economic indicators of class, both in terms of their own class identity, and in the identification of 'outsiders'. The self-identified middle class gave a more varied answer, whereby 'hard', external factors such as economic well-being and 'soft', internal factors such as cultural and behavioural indicators both have a degree of influence on their perceptions of class. They also appeared to draw distinction between what defined their own class, and what differentiated 'others': internalised factors related to earning and spending are still considered significant in underpinning their own class identity, but they cease to be important when judging another's class. Their general emphasis on cultural and symbolic factors, such as education, mannerisms and *suzhi* in being the main determinant of class identity, is consistent with Bourdieu's idea of the symbolic boundaries of class, where the class 'habitus' (Bourdieu 1973, 2000), signified through symbolic factors, such as taste, mannerisms and behaviour, are just as important as hard, objective factors in underpinning one's class position. This is not to say that the salaried class respondents are exempt from these symbolic indicators of class, just that the self-identified middle class respondents claim to be more aware of them. Whereas salaried class respondents are preoccupied with economic indicators of class, the self-identified middle class exhibit a greater awareness of so-called middle class characteristics that are both related to, and on top of, their economic well-being.

This all suggests that there is a consistent internalisation of social identities among the respondents who are independent of their economic status, as well as their perceived position in society. It raises the question of how people perceive classes, or social categories, outside of the academic context, and the significance of such popular perceptions in creating 'social groups', or classes with sociopolitical significance.

Table 2.2 How subjective class identities affect respondents' perception of class identity as a whole

Middle class	Salaried class

Most significant factors in defining own class identity

1. **Income = education***
 (68%, *n.i.* 1.61)
2. **Lifestyle beliefs**
 (58%, *n.i.* 1.38)
3. **Consumption**
 (57%, *n.i.* 1.35)
4. **Manner of speech = *guanxi***
 (51%, *n.i.* 1.22)

1. **Income**
 (82%, *n.i.* 2.2)
2. **Consumption**
 (68%, *n.i.* 1.86)

Most significant factors in differentiating others of a different class

1. **Lifestyle beliefs**
 (65%, *n.i.* 2.27)
2. **Manner of speech**
 (51%, *n.i.* 1.77)
3. **Suzhi**
 (48%, *n.i.* 1.67)

1. **Income**
 (67%, *n.i.* 2.06)
2. **Consumption**
 (51%, *n.i.* 1.57)

n.i., normalizing index.
*These factors share the same rank of significance (shown by the = sign; see Appendix).

For ease of reference, the term 'salaried class' will be used when the respondents describe their class identity as '*gongxin jieceng*'. The reason for employing 'salaried class' rather than 'working class' or even 'lower middle class' as a translated label for *gongxin jieceng* is because the key point of emphasis is on the salary, the type of income rather than the type of work one does for receiving that income. To call them working class would be confusing as they are, by sociological definition, not working class: none of them are factory workers, migrant workers, or employed in the manual labour sector. Calling them lower middle class would be suggesting that they occupy a different socioeconomic position than their self-identified middle class counterparts, which is not the case. In these cases, the difference between *gongxin jieceng* and *zhongchan jieceng* lies only in subjective self-ascription, not objective socioeconomic status. Thus, it is worth bearing in mind even the 'salaried class' label is a subjective ascription and not an objective one: it is perfectly possible for someone to have his or her salary as the sole or main source of income, yet still identify him- or herself as middle class. It is also possible for someone to have a multitude of investment options and savings, while holding a salaried position, and as long as he identifies more strongly with his salaried situation and chooses to identify himself as *gongxin jieceng*, his subjective ascription will be respected and he is henceforth called 'salaried class'. Again, it is worth noting that all of the respondents in this sample occupy objective middle class socioeconomic positions and that the discrepancy in their class identity is a subjective one.

Relative deprivation and anxieties of the 'salaried class'

For those who consider themselves salaried class, the discrepancy between their perception of their own class identity and their objective class position is not the simple result of them interpreting their class label at surface value. Instead, there is a strong internalisation of their class identity based on their limited earning power, lack of real estate ownership with investment options and a general sense of relative deprivation. This does not mean that they are in reality financially insecure or uncertain, or that they are similar to the 'precariat' who live on short term, often zero-hour contracts and low wages (Standing 2011). In contrast, they are, like their self-proclaimed middle class counterparts, in comfortable white collar occupations and hold a similarly steady income. However, they insist that the way they earned and the way they have to spend their living were more important than the absolute sum of their earnings and expenditure: as average 'salarymen', their primary expenditure items included mortgage payments, groceries, family financial commitments (such as childcare and care for elderly parents) and other items of daily maintenance. Their actual disposable income after these essential payments were made is drastically lower than their actual declared income, or even income after tax. Thus, items that were not necessary in daily life and/or unplanned for in the monthly budget were all considered 'luxuries', as they could not afford to spend on a whim. This was not the same as being unable to afford them in simple monetary terms – they could, if they had to, but without a good reason, they would not. The phenomenon of having a middle income, but not the associated high earning lifestyle was referred to as 'inflated income on paper'.

> There are a lot of salaried class like us in Ningbo. On the surface we earn a good amount of salary, but once the big expenditure is taken away from us, there is very little money left that we can control for ourselves.
>
> —*Kun*

Interestingly, whose who did consider themselves middle class did not pay nearly as much attention to their economic status, but instead emphasised their cultural and behavioural characteristics, which were built upon their economic well-being. The idea of 'money first, culture later' is also recognised by their salaried class counterparts: thus, it was not that they thought they were without *suzhi* compared to their middle class counterparts, but rather that their economic foundations are not strong enough to allow them to claim an authentic middle class lifestyle, where *suzhi* may claim prominence over money.

The acute awareness of their current way of life has led to a widespread sense of relative deprivation on the part of those who see themselves as salaried class. Table 2.3 shows that a significantly higher proportion of salaried class respondents in this sample rated their living standards as 'below average' (46 per cent), compared to their self-acknowledged middle class counterparts (8 per cent).

More importantly, Table 2.4 shows that the evidence of relative deprivation among those members of the middle class who see themselves as salaried class

Social identity of the middle class 19

Table 2.3 Subjective assessment of standards of living: overall

Overall living standards	Middle class (all)	Salaried class	Entire sample
Above average	11%	0%	5%
Average	81%	54%	68%
Below average	8%	46%	27%

Table 2.4 Subjective assessment of standards of living: breakdown

Groceries and consumables	Middle class (all)	Salaried class
Above average	13%	6%
Average	83%	76%
Below average	5%	18%
Clothing, jewellery and non-consumables	*Middle class (all)*	*Salaried class*
Above average	8%	3%
Average	79%	50%
Below average	13%	47%
Residential neighbourhoods and living quarters	*Middle class (all)*	*Salaried class*
Above average	13%	3%
Average	72%	55%
Below average	15%	42%
Mode of transport and use of private car	*Middle class (all)*	*Salaried class*
Above average	22%	6%
Average	68%	65%
Below average	10%	29%

is lowest for their groceries and consumables, followed by use of private cars, residential quarters, and clothing, jewellery and other non-consumables (18 per cent, 29 per cent, 42 per cent and 47 per cent below average, respectively). The fact that most of the salaried class respondents also considered themselves to have an average or above average living standards in their grocery shopping and car ownership shows that they are well within the objective middle class parameters; their daily comfort is guaranteed, as is ownership of private cars (an important indicator of middle class), yet they might not live in middle class neighbourhoods, and cannot afford preferential spending on non-consumables, even to be considered 'average'. In contrast, only 13 per cent of those who deemed themselves middle class considered their standards of clothing, jewellery and other non-consumables to be below average. This finding illustrates again that it is not the amount of income that determines one's perception of class position but the result of that income – how far that income will go, and what kind of lifestyle that income will bring, relative to one's peers. In the words of one respondent who, despite a yearly income of more than ¥200,000, still placed himself firmly in the salaried class category:

> I think the most representative indicator of our class is the chief makeup of our income: a working salary, and how we can spend it: not liberally.
>
> —Kun

In some ways, this is not a new phenomenon. Previous research has already suggested that an elite class with 'total capital' has squeezed the living space of the middle-middle classes, creating a much larger lower-middle class (similar to the salaried class in this study), who have a downward identification tendency due to their feelings of relative deprivation (Zhao 2004b; Sun and Guo 2013). Or perhaps they, like many others, felt both hopeful in their emancipation and hopeless in their disempowerment in the rapid expansion of urban consumerism (Davis 2005). In any case, the literal interpretation of the term 'salaried class' is as much an internalisation of their anxieties as an externalisation of their economic status.

While there is research that suggests anxiety is a characteristic middle class trait (Liu 2001), the anxiety that results from a mismatch between objective middle class position and a lack of subjective middle class identification is more pronounced. Indeed, in this sample, self-identifying salaried class respondents were notably more anxious than their middle class counterparts: only 49 per cent felt their life was content and relaxed, compared to 70 per cent of their middle class counterparts. One of the key elements underlining such anxiety was their preoccupation with the rising prices of the housing market. Many of the self-identifying salaried class respondents felt their mortgage was the key burden that held their class down. This source of anxiety is particularly prevalent among young professionals, especially men, who, unlike their parents in the state-provides-all era, have to seek housing themselves. This kind of anxiety creates a vicious cycle: the pressure on the coming-of-age young man to procure a house for marriage rises as the housing prices skyrocket, which in turn puts a greater emphasis on the young male to have a house ready before he can be considered ready for marriage. To them, having a mortgage and having a pre-paid house make a fundamental difference to their class position, because it is directly related to the amount of the real disposable income they enjoy.

Consequently, there is a noticeable preoccupation with real estate holdings and neighbourhood within the self-identifying salaried class definition of class. For them, luxury consumption on one's person (i.e. clothing, jewellery, gadgets) may not be a reliable class marker, because it is possible to forego such luxuries in order to remain low key. In contrast, it was considered illogical to compromise one's standard of living in terms of cars and homes, both of which people spend a lot of time in. Thus, not only do the salaried class appear cognisant of the difference between socially segregated communities that range in price, quality and location, but they also attest to the effect of urban middle class 'enclaves' (Tomba 2004; Pow 2009; Zhang 2012). Some identified the class of their peers based on the fact that they live close together and rent in the same area, while others felt that if they could identify one person to be unmistakably middle class, then the residents of that person's neighbourhood could all be confidently identified as such. One respondent, who was professionally involved in the advertising and marketing of new real estate developments, was keenly aware of how different neighbourhoods are marketed to different classes:

> When we try to sell houses, we'd scope out our target market, and often it's the middle class. We'd usually set the price to around 3 to 4 million, that would actually cover a huge proportion of people in this city, so we'd likely be able to sell well. I think that's what class is. Personally I can only afford a house that costs somewhere between 1.5 to 2 million, so I'm not middle class.
>
> —Kun

The very fact that he could afford a house priced at around two million CNY and yet not consider himself middle class is testament to the keen sense of anxiety and relative deprivation of the salaried class. Indeed, their understanding of class is deeply affected by the way they see themselves: lacking in means of supplemental income, thus still subject to financial instability. They are less concerned about their everyday living standards, which their working wage can provide comfortably for, but more anxious about the 'big spends', which could easily drain their savings. The inability to sustain the comfortable middle lifestyle without their working wage is what defines their subjective class identity: as their wage is their principal or only means of income, they have to continuously work hard to keep earning these wages; thus, they will remain salaried class in the most literal sense. The interpretation of class and their precarious socioeconomic position for those who identify as salaried class highlight the deep anxieties afflicting a large proportion of Chinese urban residents today: in a sense, they are truly on a 'slippery' ladder (Donnan, Bland and Burn-Murdoch 2014).

Beyond economic status: the subjective middle class

Economic well-being, or the lack thereof, was the most prominent class marker for the salaried class. Instead, the self-identified middle class emphasised the 'soft', cultural and behavioural aspects, and saw class to be less quantifiable, although no less distinct. While they also acknowledged their material wealth to be an important class marker, they did not fixate on them the same way the salaried class respondents did. However, there can be no doubt that the luxuries of actually being middle class is dependent on one's middle, or even upper middle socioeconomic position, as the latter is assumed as an achieved given, before the former can be discussed and used in reference to the individual's middle class identity.

While traditional economic indicators such as income, occupation and consumption clearly played a role in their identity formation, it was clear that those who identified themselves as middle class approached each of these issues from a different angle compared to their salaried class counterparts. First, for the middle class, occupation was also their career; they take pride in their workplace, which is often top in the field, and consider their peers to be bright and dynamic. In contrast, those who considered themselves salaried class made little to no mention of their workplace or their colleagues; for them, occupation was simply a job, a means to get a salary. Even for the younger generation, who saw potential in their class improving, work at the starting point of their career was no more than a daily toil, an office position that one could not distinguish from one cubicle to the other. Thus, occupation was an integral part of middle class identity, but just work for those who identified themselves as salaried class.

Second, the consumption choices of the subjective middle class are far more conscious, hence more reflexive of their perceived class identity. Whereas the self-identifying salaried class felt constrained by their limited disposable income, the self-identifying middle class had more liberty to purchase non-essential goods, or pursue a specific lifestyle that they felt reflected their social identities. More common in the middle-aged respondents who are well established in their careers, the middle class lifestyle was deliberate, with an emphasis on quality, as expressed below.

> I think I count as middle class because I pursue a quality lifestyle. I have hobbies, I exercise, and I adopt a healthy regimen as a way of life. When I buy things, I buy things that would match my identity. My bags, my electronics, things I use are usually big and international brands ... I wouldn't put random food in my mouth just like I wouldn't put random clothes on my body, or hang a random bag off my arm. They are all important to me.
>
> —*Aline*

The significance of consumption for middle class identity is a well-researched subject. The type of goods one consumes, the brand and the venue can all be important symbols of social status, which helps to form the middle class habitus (Anagnost 2008; Cartier 2008; Hanser 2008). The point worth making here is that middle class consumption is seen above all as a conscious choice, thus in part embodying perceived financial freedom: only those who felt free to choose and alter their own consumption habits considered themselves middle class. Indeed, because the respondents shared similar levels of objective income, there was a significant overlap of shopping and dining spheres between the subjective salaried class and the middle class, clustered towards the middle of the spectrum (Table 2.5 and Figure 2.1). Thus, unlike the difference between someone with a low income and someone with a high income, an observable distinction could not be made based on where one did visit, but rather needs to be drawn between where they did *not*.

When dining out, very few self-identified middle class respondents would visit restaurants that cost less than ¥50 per head, whereas no salaried class respondent would visit a luxury establishment that would cost more than ¥500. Similarly, whereas 42 per cent of salaried class respondents prefer to visit farmers' markets

Table 2.5 Which shopping venues do you frequent?

Frequented shopping venue (multiple choice)	Salaried class	Middle class
Local food markets, roadside dealers	42%	15%
Local chain supermarkets (*Sanjiang, Xinjiangxia*, etc.)	79%	73%
International chain supermarkets (Tesco, Carrefour, Walmart, etc.)	80%	88%
High-end supermarkets (O'le, Marks & Spencers, etc.)	7%	13%
Online shopping (Taobao, etc.)	56%	43%

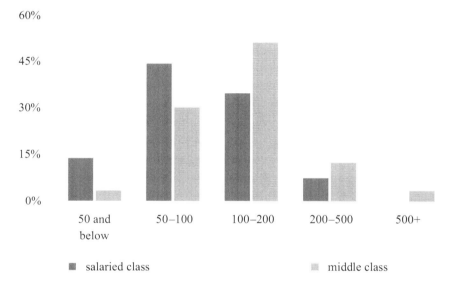

Figure 2.1 Average spending when eating out (¥RMB per head)

and roadside stalls for their food shopping, only 15 per cent of self-identified middle class would, while the reverse pattern is true for high-end supermarkets. This kind of stratified consumer behaviour, similar to what Hanser observed, is also due to the social practice of calculability, of establishing risk and value in the marketplace (Hanser 2010). Whereas the salaried class felt roadside stalls and farmers' markets offered them cheaper produce, the middle class respondents felt they could afford to forego these places to 'save time on bargaining' and 'ensure baseline quality' in their goods. Similarly, whereas self-identifying salaried class respondents joked that they 'did not even know which direction the doors opened onto the road' in some of the more expensive establishments, the middle class respondents felt they could afford the atmosphere, service and quality some of these establishments offered on occasion. Again, the emphasis was less on the actual goods and services that they consumed, but rather on the act of choosing: being middle class meant that one had more freedom to enjoy a wider social sphere. Making this choice was not only the result of the individual's economic well-being but also of self-perception of economic well-being: it is not a simple question of whether the individual could afford the goods and services, but whether they could afford it as a part of a lifestyle, which in turn feeds into class identity.

Beyond these symbols of economic status, the subjective middle class also placed a greater emphasis on the idea of cultural and behavioural criteria of class, which their self-identifying salaried class counterparts did not preoccupy themselves with. Education was an important underpinning of middle class identity, although less in terms of certified education, and more about the act of becoming learned, which is often considered responsible for the individual's change in *suzhi* and *qizhi* (气质, disposition – the air with which one holds oneself). Although not referred to explicitly, this idea of change in one's mannerisms and behaviour has apparent Confucian roots, in the age-old idea of being a *junzi*, a gentleman, and *li*, the ritual and proper conduct of society. Having money is not considered enough: only when a person also strives to better him- or herself can he or she be considered to have attained superior social status, or in this case, the middle class. This transformation is a holistic process; it is built on economic foundations, but requires also substantial changes in one's cognitive outlook.

It is unsurprising that the emphasis of the middle class on symbolic factors are particularly strong when they are differentiating those 'others' who meet the economic criteria for that class, but are found lacking in other aspects. Economic factors might be fundamental to pin down their own class identity, but simply being similar on a material level was not enough, or indeed relevant, for them to associate with someone as a member of their class, as expressed below:

> I believe I am middle class by income, but I would never identify with another person, or think of them as middle class, simply because of their occupation or income. That has to come from something else – the way they behave, their mannerisms, their ways of thought.
>
> —*Jinying*

Therefore, while income is still seen as the key foundation of their own class identity, it is not considered a reliable frame of reference to judge another's class. Here the soft indicator such as one's values, outlook on life, and the state of one's career all contributed towards the 'feeling' that would help to identify how someone is perceived in society, not just how well off someone is. Thus, class identity is also something ingrained, a distillation of one's past experience and current circumstances, something fundamental that cannot be replicated for someone without similar background or experiences; it is often 'felt' more than 'seen', a sense of belonging and accordant behaviour rather than a checklist of required items.

Social identity of the middle class 25

> … Your economic position reflects the way you dress and the goals you pursue, while your social position reflects in the way you speak and do things … you can't pretend to be some class when you are not.
>
> —Jane

Furthermore, as these 'soft' factors were often unquantifiable, it was also easier to tell who was not one's own class, rather than who was: one respondent gave a negative example of her neighbour, who, despite being well-off and leading a quality life, is deemed to be un-middle class because of his/her lack of regard for others.

> There is this family that lives in my apartment block, they are rich and they eat well, but they never put their rubbish away and they pile their personal stuff into communal areas. I don't call them middle class, they are just parvenus.
>
> —Aline

The idea of *bao'fa'hu* (parvenu: the *nouveau riche* or 'rich upstart') is frequently used to identify those with enough money to be considered middle or high income, but lack the necessary education and learned quality to match (Lei 2003). One's manner of speech, clothing, and public behaviour can all be used to distinguish a 'rich upstart' from a true middle class, and these factors, more than anything, determine whether a person is accepted into a specifically middle class social circle, as expressed below:

> I wouldn't socialise with a parvenu, just as I wouldn't want to go out with someone with just a primary school education.
>
> —Jessie

This distinction between crude money and cultured middle class is in part reflective of China's Confucian past, and in part a product of China's rapid economic growth in the last decades. Traditionally, the Confucian social structure has always valued scholars above merchants, education over accumulation of private wealth, in that the former strove for the betterment of self and society, whereas the latter focused only on profit without even the production of physical goods (Reischauer and Fairbank 1960). While aspects of the Confucian value system remain influential to this day, the rapid socioeconomic transformations of China in the last century saw an overturn of traditional routes of social mobility, along with social structure, where the pace of personal wealth accumulation could now conceivably outgrow the pace of accumulation for one's education and wisdom. This mistmatch between the rate of economic accumulation and education attainment after the reform results in the disparaging attitude between class position, which still largely rests upon economic foundations, and class identity, which extends beyond monetary terms. Consequently, a stratified intra-class habitus forms, which is used mostly to distinguish one group's superiority over the other. Just as the late Ming elites once produced manuals of 'taste' in an attempt to redefine and re-enforce necessary correlations between status, taste and consumption, so that they could distinguish themselves from the newly wealthy who were overcoming the previously rigid social barriers and threatening their elite status (Clunas 1991), those who identified themselves as middle class in today's China also hastened to separate themselves from crude money, whom they see as undeserving of the middle class label. For them, the distinction that really underpins their class identity is social and cultural in origin, not economic, which is responsible first and foremost for their class position.

Economic security and cultural superiority: the imagined 'middle class'

Despite different points of emphasis, in constructing their respective class identities, both classes use similar imaginings of the ideal 'middle class', whose cultured lifestyle rests upon strong economic foundations. Before one could discuss the intangible quality of one's education and mannerisms, one must be securely financially established: sometimes the imagined middle income line is drawn so high that any academic calculations seem inappropriate by comparison. One respondent said:

> To be middle class, first you have to earn half a million RMB a year, posttax. You should have two houses, one in the city, another in the rural area, a retreat. You should have two cars, and a floating capital of two million. This is roughly what the senior executives in my firm earn. I use them as an example not only because of who they are in my firm but also who they represent as a whole, in my field of career, and also society in general. These people are definitely seen as middle class, not just because I see them as such.
>
> —Kun

The key here is that not only did he believe that these values represented the middle class criteria for him, but they were also how he believed society would judge the middle class by – indeed, a quick Internet search turns up numerous uncredited sources of middle class incomes reaching as high as a yearly income of ¥250,000, nearly ten times higher than the national average income, and nearly three times as high as the 'high income' line frequently cited in academia. This finding further suggests that there is a notable discrepancy between how the middle class is perceived, and how the middle class is believed to be perceived, by the very members who could otherwise be categorised as middle class.

Contrary to the scholarly definition of middle income, the perceived minimum economic criteria for middle class seem at first glance arbitrary and unfounded. However, there is a consistent cognitive reason behind such imaginings, which is reflected in the prevalent idea that a middle class life is only possible when one is 'warm, full and with enough to spare', with the emphasis on the word 'spare'. This interpretation is not simply a reiteration of the Engel's Coefficient, which some studies refer to as the marker for middle class (Zhou 2008). Here, the imagined 'necessities for subsistence' is a much wider category, which includes food, shelter (thus by extension any necessary housing mortgages, present or future), potential health care, childcare and elderly care expenditures, and other aspects where social welfare is limited. Indeed, the phrase denotes a certain sense of freedom from material anxieties, which, in face of China's rapidly changing socioeconomic environment, is perceived to require much more than the national average income.

It is within these contexts that the ability to afford a certain level of enjoyment in life and leisure pursuits is seen as important to middle class identity. Quality consumption, ability to travel and send children abroad for education, intellectual pursuits, hobbies and ambition were all part of the 'financially worry-free lifestyle', which distinguishes them from those who prioritise financial needs above else. The common denominator in all the factors was the quality of life a middle class person is supposed to enjoy – above and beyond what is needed to survive in the city, but all the extras that would enrich one's life experience, thus positively affecting one's mannerisms and behaviour.

As a result, there is a certain level of cultural expectation attached to the concept of middle class, which is commonly recognised, and corresponds with existing research that suggests post-reform China has seen a shift from the focus on political and economic capital to human capital as a key element in the path to increased social status (Hsu 2007), and that the middle class is instrumental in both consuming and producing the 'cultural difference' discourse of *suzhi* (Anagnost 2008). The idea is that the middle class comfortable lifestyle and adequate education should be reflected by being 'dignified' and 'well-versed' in culture, having a 'sense of order in their lives', hence being 'a stabilising force in society'. This ideal middle class image coincides neatly with China's official middle class discourse, which incorporates the idea of *suzhi* and harmony in order to maintain legitimacy and sociopolitical stability. In a sense, their imagining of a middle class person is a 'social stabiliser', rather than a driver of democratic change. Therefore, the ideal middle class citizen is one who has careful planning of his finances, enjoys a healthy balance of work and life, allows both material and spiritual luxuries without interrupting normal day-to-day routine, and through these activities would inspire a greater sense of cohesion in society. To achieve this level of equilibrium, the individual needs all of the factors just described: money, education and life experience.

Of all the criteria outlined, money was seen as the most important, but it was also the easiest to achieve: thus, a common distinction is made between the rich upstarts and the middle class. Here, the major differences lie not only in their education and cultured behaviour but also how they arrived at their fortune, whether it was through moral and respectable means. Thus, social status – the other important cornerstone of middle class identity – is not simply acquired through accumulation of wealth (Zang 2008). Individuals with success in innovative fields, and those seen as taking certain levels of social responsibility such as Steve Jobs and Bill Gates were considered to be inspiring examples (although the extent to which either of these examples can be considered middle class is debatable). Those with inherited money were accepted, though less respected, as the respondents were often dismissive of their success, choosing to believe that they most likely owed it to their family background. The most frowned upon, however, are those who profit from land holdings; they, like the mercantile class in earlier Confucian ideology, were seen as 'gaining from nothing'. A typical complaint reads as follows:

> Some people become rich by being landlords. You know how the government compensates peasants with many houses for requisitioning their land, these people would just rent out their houses and they become rich without even having to work for it. The prominent real estate tycoons exploit this system even more so. Real estate is the simplest, but least moral way to become rich in Chinese society nowadays. I really don't want to include these people in the middle and upper class of society ... it's like they are gaining from nothing. There is no contribution to society, instead they just widen the poverty gap, and worsen the Gini coefficient.
>
> —*Ophelia*

Similarly, people are judged by how their behaviour changes after acquiring their fortune. Again, the sentiment of 'being a productive member of society' and 'contributing towards societal development as a whole' is very important, or just the need to better oneself. It is expected that with their improved economic status, they must also seek to elevate their cultural awareness in order to qualify to be called middle class. The peasants who 'burn away their fortune on the mah-jong table', for example, would not make the cut, neither would the office drone who continues to 'waste her day away on the computer watching Korean soaps'. Various stereotypes were attached to these supposed parvenus, and unless their behaviour broke out of the stereotypical labels assigned to their previous class role, they were not accepted as middle class.

Whereas the respondents drew a keen distinction between parvenus and legitimate members of the middle class, not many could adequately explain the difference between salaried class and middle class, as they imagined it. Aside from the interpretation drawn from the working salary, those who considered themselves salaried class often could not pinpoint the exact difference that lies between themselves and their imagined middle class counterparts. They certainly did not believe they were culturally inferior, or even that this was a valid point of comparison between them and their middle class counterparts, suggesting that the cultural distinction only becomes significant as a form of class habitus after the economic criteria are met. Thus, the relationship between the economic and cultural criteria is one of superposition and interdependence: income is seen as the prerequisite, and culture as the defining point of middle class identity. Only those with spare money can pursue the cultured aspect of middle class experience, which is distilled in one's *suzhi*, as an aggregation of beliefs, attitude and behaviour. Without adequate income, the cultivation of culture is difficult, and without culture, riches alone only make a parvenu. In acquiring the middle class label, income is simply the entry requirement; one cannot hope to graduate as middle class without passing as 'cultured' and 'with *suzhi*' in the eyes of the beholder.

Middle class identity and subjectivity

There is clearly a disjuncture between the subjective perceptions of class, and its objective, socioeconomic or sociopolitical conditions among this particular sample of middle class respondents. Most notably, being categorised as middle class objectively does not necessarily reflect a corresponding subjective middle class identity, as nearly half of the 'objective' middle class preferred to identify themselves as salaried class. The emphasis was that it is not the sum of income that determines one's class identity, as advocated by the majority of scholarly research on the middle class, but the type: from *where* and *how* one receives one's income is more important than *how much*. Whereas the working wage could afford one with a mediocre lifestyle, being middle class requires something more: the financial stability of having extra sources of income that are nondependent on one's day-to-day work, and the cultured lifestyle that can only be built upon a steady and stable economic foundation. The former is the economic prerequisite of middle class, whereas the latter is the psychological prerequisite; without a conscious attempt at adjusting one's behaviour to be educated, cultured and mannered, one can only be parvenu in the eyes of others.

Thus, subjective class identity is often determined through means of exclusion rather than inclusion – what they believed they are not rather than what they believed they are. This is not only true of middle class respondents but also their salaried class counterparts, suggesting that perhaps class boundaries are more perception than socioeconomic reality. Indeed, the point was also raised that class as a concept is comparative, for the identification of the middle class even more so. Class is defined subjectively via self-assessment and peer observation; thus, class is often seen as something tangible that is within the context of people's environment, not as an arbitrary line drawn by simple statistical analysis.

These highly subjective answers highlight the importance of endogenous belief in the formation of class identity rather than exogenous definition. People's perceptions of what class and middle class are, and are not, are both extremely relevant in identifying their class peers and non-peers, regardless of whether their understanding adheres to scholarly definitions. China's socioeconomic reform since the 1980s have led to the decline of political ideas of class, whereas the inequalities between social classes have prevailed. Thus, class is no longer seen as a political marker, but rather a social phenomenon: the principal difference being that the former is often ascribed, whereas the latter is observed. As such, class in China functions more like a form of social identity, the formation of which is not only dependent on how the members view themselves but also how the members view outsiders (Moloney and Walker 2007; Tajfel 2010). This process of observation, comparison, interaction and adaption is particularly important for the middle class, who, by virtue of their 'middleness', needs to be contextualised in order to exist. While the imagined middle class do exist in people's perception, its exact definers are ambiguous, and often unquantifiable, and its boundaries not precise. More often than not, such imaginings serve to affirm people in their lack of middle class characteristics, rather than being used to validate their middle class-ness. The number of objective middle class in China might appear to be on the rise, but the actual number of those who actively identify with their *middle class* identity, and are not just ascribable to the middle income or middle of society, and behave accordingly, is likely to be considerably smaller. As they also define their class identity through means of exclusion rather than inclusion, intra-class cohesion is likely weak as well. It is possible for members of the same group to each identify with 'middle class' as a group label themselves, but not with each other; if this is so, then the emergence of a coherent Chinese middle class sharing identifiable characteristics, and capable of any class action might still be far on the horizon. By implication, a meaningful middle class who could conceivably challenge China's socio-political status quo are also unlikely to arise out of such a fragmented group. If we are to understand the Chinese middle class better as a social and political phenomenon, then, research needs to pay more attention to the intrinsic cognitive processes that affect their beliefs, as well as the socioeconomic processes that affect their position. The following chapters explore how these respondents conceive the sociopolitical environment in which they live, and how this perception affects their values and behaviour.

3 Between the state and the market

One of the key factors differentiating the Chinese middle class and its global, especially Western, counterparts is its relationship with the state. Those scholars who reject the application of modernisation theory to China typically refer to the middle class as having vested interest in the state, as being the winners of economic reform in the last forty years, and to the fact that there is limited space for civil participation in China that would allow the middle class to occupy a position outside the state (Huang 1993; Brook and Frolic 1997). Furthermore, scholars such as Tu Weiming have long since argued that China's Confucian past gives rise to a paternalistic state, whereby state-society relations reflect that of a father-son relationship than a social contract typical in modern societies (Pye 1991; Tu, Harrison and Huntington 2000; Fairbrother 2013). However, research has also shown that the middle class are more critical of government performance than other classes (Zhang 2008), which feeds the idea that the middle class in authoritarian states will gradually grow out of its dependency on the existing institutions and seek reform (Li 2008b). This chapter examines how the middle class respondents view the state, especially in terms of state performance and responsibilities in the area of welfare.

Over the last three decades, China's socioeconomic policies have undergone a major reform with a neoliberal tendency. With the gradual opening of the private sector also came a reduction in government's role in welfare, the replacement of the socialist direct-planned universal welfare provision with a redistributive welfare model, an increase in emphasis of individual responsibility in public discourse and a decrease in public provision of services in many fields (Guan 2000). On the one hand, this change in policy paved the way for the rise of the urban middle class, who embody the 'self-made' discourse; on the other hand, the rolling back of the state in welfare areas also poses risks to the same middle class, who, unlike their Western counterparts, are very much on a slippery ladder (Donnan, Bland, and Burn-Murdoch 2014). Indeed, widespread dissatisfaction with the current public institutions such as health care, education and pension is a key impact and concern of the ongoing socioeconomic restructuring, with the rise of privatised alternatives as a part of the debate. Whether the middle class subscribe to the idea of privatisation of public services will be crucial to this debate, as they are most likely to be the core consumers of such privatised alternatives.

32 *Between the state and the market*

All of these factors come together to offer an interesting picture of the welfare attitudes of the Chinese middle class: on the one hand, they are advocates of individual responsibility and privatised choice; on the other hand, they are also more trusting of state involvement in welfare and public services, and recognise the need for the state to provide a social 'safety net' for the disadvantaged. Unlike the self-interest/moral inclination dichotomy posed by their counterparts in the West, it emerges in this chapter that the welfare attitudes of these middle class respondents are influenced heavily by their assessment of the role and nature of the state, which is seen as impartial and non-profit driven, hence better suited to the task of public service provision, in contrast to the private sector, which is seen as amoral and elitist, and thus only able to act as an addition, not as an alternative. Therefore, despite having heavy criticisms towards the current performance of key public service institutions, these middle class respondents are only welcoming of privatisation as a form of public sector diversification, but not as a replacement.

Personal income tax: 'honest worker's burden'

Despite the fact that China's state revenue depends mostly on indirect taxes (Jing and Ximing 2013), for many of the respondents, having personal income tax (PIT) deducted from their monthly pay slip is the most direct interaction they have with the government on a regular basis, and the most discernible way for them to contribute towards state coffers. Having a progressive tax scale that starts at 3 per cent for a monthly taxable income of ¥1,500 and topping at 45 per cent for ¥80,000 taxable income per month, the PIT band for someone with a middle class income of ¥87,500 is roughly around 20 per cent. Of all of the surveyed respondents, very few thought that the current PIT scale was reasonable (8 per cent), and more than 50 per cent thought it was too high. Nearly a third were ambivalent with regard to the question. A closer look reveals that more of those with a higher income and middle class self-identification thought PIT was too high: the former perhaps less surprising than the latter, as it has been seen that among those surveyed, objective criteria such as income do not necessarily correlate with middle class identity.

Table 3.1 How do you view the current personal income tax in China?

	Percentage who thought the current PIT was too high (n=258)	*Percentage who thought the current PIT was too low (n=258)*	*Percentage who thought the current PIT was just right (n=258)*	*Not sure/ no answer (n=258)*
Middle income (37k–87.5k)	50	11	11	28
High income (>87.5k)	66	4	5	24
Salaried class	52	9	6	33
Middle class	66	5	1	18
Overall	53	10	8	29

When interviewed, those who identified themselves as middle class all thought that the salaried class were taxed the heaviest. Some of the self-identified salaried class respondents voiced similar concerns, although they all pointed out that the unfairness mostly lies in the fact that the rich are under-taxed. This finding suggests that the middle class respondents do not see themselves as rich – indeed, only 3 per cent of this sample were willing to categorise themselves as rich – and the unfairness that they feel is not a result of themselves being taxed too heavily in absolute terms but rather the idea that their richer counterparts are not being taxed enough. This finding is consistent with Li Chunling's study in 2006 that found similar heightened sense of social injustice among the middle class (Li 2013), which she believed was 'observatory' rather than 'experienced'. The results of this study also support this hypothesis, as most respondents described such injustices in overall and general tones, rather than in specific and personal terms.

Among those interviewed, both Lu and Aline thought that tax evasion was a serious problem in China, and the ability of the rich to do so underscores the fundamental inequality in this area. They argued that the act of paying tax is not upheld as a virtue in China, and that the sense of 'obligation' and 'duty' is weak, so that tax evasion is not seen as a crime, nor do the rich feel guilty about it. Often, the act of evasion is neither conscious nor active: 'grey income' is mentioned frequently as a major source of income for the rich and the privileged (the civil servants being the key category), which is virtually un-taxable. The lack of accountability and transparency in government operations also meant that taxpayers have very little say or even knowledge over where their money is being channelled to, or if it has gone into private pockets. If, and when, misconduct is exposed, taxpayers often cannot do anything about it, as it is seen as the social 'norm'. Aline thought that this kind of uncertainty possibly justifies the act of tax evasion in the eyes of the rich, as it is essentially a form of breakdown in social contract.

On the other hand, respondents claimed that because the salaried class normally operate by the books, the state will most regularly tax them. There is little mention of virtue or upstandingness involved: instead, the salaried class automatically loses out because their income is transparent, and lacking the means and the resources for tax avoidance or evasion, they are stuck with the heavy duty of supporting the state coffers. However, the respondents did not think they would evade tax if the means were made available; rather, the idea was that they, unlike the rich, do not have a choice – to them, the cost of tax evasion is much lower for the rich and the benefit is much greater, while the same cannot be said for their case. Aline describes that sense of being punished for acting as an upstanding citizen as follows:

> Personally, I don't feel the tax rate is fair. I know people who are richer than me who pay less in tax. I pay several tens of thousands a year, but I lose out if I'm not willing to evade tax or go for those grey, law-skirting activities. It's like being punished for being a good citizen and an honest worker.

Furthermore, many salaried class respondents felt that the current tax scheme is too arbitrary, and does not consider varying circumstances. Both Lily and Kun mentioned the inadequacies of the individual tax: they raised the concern that if only one person is working in a household of five, it would be unfair to levy the same amount of tax on that person, compared to another individual who might earn a similar income, but does not have any dependents. Kun further argued that the PIT band should be considered as a part of the wider welfare scheme, according to circumstance:

> I think income under ¥10,000 a month should not be taxed. That's the bare minimum you need for yourself to make a good life in the city, really … I think the amount of taxes we pay should be decided on circumstance: for example, right now my wife and I live alone, and we can afford to pay a bit more tax, that's fine. When we have a child, can we pay a bit less? When we have two children, even more so? What if my parents can't afford pension for themselves, can further tax breaks be made? But I think it's not practical in China.

When Kun argued for ¥10,000 a month as a bare survival income, he was also considering the consumption standards of the people in Ningbo, which in their eyes are on a par with first-tier cities such as Beijing or Shanghai. Regional differences were highlighted as a major source of tax inequality: while tax bands are universal across the country, the same amount of income could mean considerably different living standards in different cities. Jessie complains that a monthly income of ¥3,500–5,000, already taxable at approximately 10 per cent, is barely enough for survival in a third-tier city, and nearly impossible to live on in first-tier cities. She tallied an account in the following manner:

> Let me do the math for you. If I earn ¥3000 a month, at least ¥700 of this is going for the rent, and that's just a single room in a shared house. Even if I eat in the canteen, this is around ¥20 a meal, so that's ¥600 for lunch. Food is not cheap in the markets nowadays – I probably need another ¥600 for dinner and breakfast, and I need to go out with friends sometimes, which adds another ¥500. That's ¥2000 gone, easy. What about my commute? Red packets for friends who marry? A few entertainment options like going to the cinema? Do I get to buy new clothes? What if I catch a cold and was prescribed antibiotics? I have no 'padding' left to make me feel safe. And ¥3000 is already an acceptable salary for many.

Not only is ¥3,000 a month (the average urban income for Ningbo residents) not enough in their eyes but double that amount brings new sources of worry: many respondents argued that once they spend a few years climbing the corporate ladder, they will be pressured to marry and buy a house, which will mean that any salary increase goes straight towards the mortgage payment. After that comes kids, and the 'milk powder money' they must set aside to make sure their children have a competitive start, and the cycle repeats. There is very few 'padding', as Jessie called it, around their income, which allows them luxuries and a sense of safety in life. This kind of reasoning further highlights the subjective, and observatory, nature of their relative deprivation, and their anxiety in trying to 'survive' in the city with an already higher than average income.

The respondents also drew attention to the fact that in China, information on valued added taxes and service taxes is not as clear as they ought to be. Japan and America were given as examples where the consumer is briefed very clearly on the amount of tax he or she would pay in each transaction, no matter how small, whereas in China, unless it was a major purchase such as a house or a car, the respondents felt they had 'no idea how much they would pay or what the taxes will be used for'. The lack of transparency further undermines their sense of tax paying as a duty, as they do not feel it is a well-balanced agreement or contract. In the end, Kun summarises his disappointment as follows:

> The way I see it, the amount of tax we are paying is rising with China's GDP. The only problem is, our living standards aren't.

It is worth noting here that despite PIT being the primary method for income redistribution in society, few respondents thought of it in these terms: instead, they saw PIT as a payment for public goods and services, and often justified their dissatisfaction for the current services by arguing that they did not have 'good value for the money', or that they felt the usage was not accountable or transparent enough. This kind of attitude is particularly prevalent in the area of health care and education.

Health care: 'Sharp class conflict'

Like many other areas, China's healthcare system has undergone profound market reforms since 1978. One of the key changes is the way health care is financed: instead of flexible cost reimbursement, sectors are given block grants and are encouraged to make their own revenue, and surpluses can be retained (Ma, Lu and Quan 2008). Health insurance coverage was also replaced by medical saving accounts, whereby the employer pays a fixed amount for partial coverage of medical costs, and the employee picks up the tab for the remaining expenses. As a result, although the percentage of GDP spending on health has increased from 4.1 per cent to 4.8 per cent from 1991 to 2000, the total percentage of government spending in health care has shrunk from 22 per cent to 14 per cent, while individual spending on health care has increased from 38 per cent to 60 per cent (Liu 2004). As Liu wrote: 'Access to health care in China is now ruled by the ability to pay', a trend that is felt keenly by those surveyed in this study.

There is an overwhelming sense of dissatisfaction with the current healthcare system, as more than two-thirds (77 per cent) of those surveyed were mostly dissatisfied, or very dissatisfied, with the system. Very few were satisfied with the system: less than 1 per cent (0.8 per cent). There is a widespread grievance that market reforms have changed health care from a 'basic needs welfare service' to 'another monetising tool', which, in the direst circumstances, 'puts people's lives at risk'. Yet, while research has shown that one of the key failings in the post-1978 healthcare reform was due to the uncoordinated policies between financing, pricing and organisation, i.e. a mismatch between top-down government controlled structure and a bottom-up user fee supported operation (Hsiao 1995), most of the respondents placed a heavier blame on market mechanisms and 'human greed', rather than pointed to the inadequacies in the role of the government and the state. As a result, two-thirds of the respondents still preferred the state ownership of hospitals, and very few wished for most or complete privatisation (5 per cent). Interestingly, a larger proportion of those who considered themselves to be part of the salaried class preferred stronger state involvement in health care (68 per cent) as opposed to their self-identified middle class counterparts (51 per cent), whereas their dissatisfaction towards the system remained ubiquitous. There is also a stronger preference for mixed ownership among the self-identified middle class respondents, as shown in Table 3.2.

What is notable is that by 'mixed ownership', the respondents who were interviewed all interpreted it as 'a mix of state-owned hospitals *and* private-owned hospitals', instead of mixed ownership of a single hospital. They expressed a desire for a dual-accessibility system, where state-owned hospitals would provide a social safety net for the masses, while those who can afford medical care should have the option of going to the private-owned hospitals that might offer better patient experience. Indeed, the key difference between those who preferred stronger state management in health care and those who accepted mixed and private alternatives was the rationale behind how best to improve the system: most salaried class respondents positioned themselves as consumers for the state-owned hospitals; hence, they placed a heavy emphasis on the role of the state in upholding public service performance, while their middle class counterparts felt that a degree of privatisation would be beneficial as an addition to the state's effort in reforming the public sector. Above all, privatisation was seen as a tool that should be utilised by the state, rather than replace the state, which explains why so few felt complete privatisation independent of the state was the answer.

The dual-accessibility system the respondents argued for can already be observed at its infancy stage in much of urban China, as reform also saw the entry of private, for-profit hospitals, accounting for 13.8 per cent of all hospitals and 72 per cent of all clinics in China in 2004 (Ma, Lu and Quan 2008). In Ningbo,

Table 3.2 In your opinion, ownership of the healthcare system should be... (n=258)

	% prefer state ownership	*% prefer privatisation*	*% prefer mixed ownership*
Salaried class	68	4	29
Middle class	51	6	43
Overall	62	5	33

the respondents acknowledged that private hospitals are gaining popularity in offering better patient experience in non-critical operations, such as dentistry and annual physical checkups. However, due to the hospital rating system in China, most of the top tier hospitals – tertiary level first class hospitals – are still state owned, and it is those hospitals that attract the best talents, largest sums of funding and largest influx of patients. Thus, despite better service, private hospitals are believed to be no real match for state-owned hospitals in terms of medical expertise. In its current state, private hospitals are associated with 'shady procedures', where people went to 'treat things they want to treat off the books', as expressed below:

> Apart from the physical checkup centres, all the private hospitals you see blaring ads on TVs don't look legit … all they seem to do is abortions, treat STDs or something embarrassing like that. I don't trust it … but if we can better regulate it and improve its quality of care, then they would relieve much pressure off the state owned hospitals.
>
> —*Abbey*

Many of the respondents, especially the self-identified salaried class, believed the rich, with their access to special relationships (*guanxi*) and invisible social capital, are dominating medical resources in state hospitals, robbing the poor of their chance at adequate and timely medical care. The increase in private health care would allow a channel for the rich to exert their wealth at a locale other than those visited by the majority of the population, hence reducing conflict and unfairness. Ophelia, who has had firsthand experience in the medical system due to her father's chronic illness, described the current battle over resources as follows:

> the poor cannot afford health care while the rich can afford a suite in the same hospital. I've heard cases where the rich goes to get blood transfusions for 'nutritional benefits', while the poor cannot afford lifesaving blood even if they badly need it…. The most pressing problem lies in the cost. Doctors earn money by prescribing things their patient may or may not need, and their attitude is often despicable, because they are overworked, have quotas to fill, and do not seem to care. It's all, 'cough up if you want to be treated, if not, who's next.' The conflict is not only there, it's very sharp.

As people's experience with the healthcare system is often personal, their opinion of the system often differed according to their personal experiences. Respondents like Ophelia and Yamei, who have had firsthand, often long-term experience in the system either because of personal or family situations, responded with more vehemence and emotions than those who confessed they had not needed the healthcare system as much. Consequently, the respondents' opinions on health care are far more intimate than their opinions on other topics. For middle-aged respondents such as Abbey, their desire for a dual accessibility system is largely the result of firsthand experience of being overwhelmed by the hospital queues, while people like Jane and William arrived at a similar proposal through observation. Although they have had little experience dealing with hospitals themselves, their study abroad experiences have made them question the validity of nationalised health care (with the case of the UK's National Health Service often used as a negative example), while they remained cautious towards the idea of complete privatisation. Thus, they have also arrived at the decision that a mixed ownership would fare better for the country. Jane outlined her position in a calm, rational way:

> I think the state should only pay the medical bills for those who also pay their taxes. Also the state shouldn't pay directly, there should be a mediator between the government and the healthcare system, which would be more readily accepted by the public. Like the insurance companies in America – everybody makes money, and government won't have to get a bad reputation because of management.

The elderly were more adamant on state involvement in health care, in what they saw as a crucial component of public services. Both Yamei and Junhui expressed a deep mistrust towards the idea of privatisation, claiming that all 'business owners' were makers of 'dirty money'. Junhui argued:

> Public services should never be privatised. When the state controls public services, it's a form of welfare. When the private sector controls it, it is for profit. Even if privatisation would offer more of a choice, it's not worth it.

The idea that the private owned is for the selfish profit and the state owned is for the selfless greater good is no doubt a remnant of their lived historical past, where private business owners were sworn class enemies of the public. Nevertheless, their memory of the socialist past did not lead them to place demands on the state: while Yamei and Junhui tentatively expressed a desire for the state to take care of their medical bills so that they will not have excessive worries in their life, their attitude made it clear that they saw the state as a benevolent father, and any form of welfare protection was welcomed, but not demanded. Their advanced age and status as a pensioner may have something to do with their relatively meek attitude: they had lived through a time where the state provided everything in their lives, but the idea of provision is not related to the idea of rights.

Their younger counterparts are more rights-conscious in this regard: many younger respondents invoked their rights to a state-paid healthcare system, because of their tax-paying status. Indeed, for some, their discontent with the current welfare scheme is intricately linked with their attitude towards tax in the previous question: they felt that their tax money was not being used to their benefit in areas of health care and welfare, but instead it was going to 'face constructions' (vanity project) so that the state can boast about its economic prowess. Whether their subjective assessment is true is another matter – the significance remains that they were more aware of the highly visible state-funded projects that they deemed to have little relevance to their actual lives. The lack of transparency in government expenditure contributed considerably towards their sense of dissatisfaction, since they felt the state was not delivering adequately on their end of the social 'agreement'. Aline asked imploringly:

> They all say the state is like our father. How would you feel if your parents spent all their money on a shiny new car, instead of looking after you?

Negative media portrayal and hearsay also add to the observed sense of injustice in health care. The respondents highlighted that not only does the media focus on medical lawsuits exacerbate the already strained doctor-patient relationship but sometimes the media appeal for private donations and public charity calls also raise the question about state inaction. Nevertheless, the emphasis remains that the state must take the primary role in reforming health care, whether it is due to respondents' sense of entitlement as taxpayers, or because of their fundamental mistrust of the private sector.

Two of the interviewed respondents, Kosei and Lu, were intimately familiar with the medical profession, and provided illuminating views from the other side. Coming from a family of doctors, Kosei's answers shed light on the deeply embedded *guanxi* networks surrounding the simple act of seeking medical care. Her main complaint about the system inequality is aimed at the way doctors are treated – as a patient, she admitted that she never had to queue to see a specialist, and her medical bills would be largely reimbursed by her workplace. This admission stands in stark contrast to what some of the other respondents have suggested, where the long queues and the lack of reimbursement were key issues in their dissatisfaction. In a way, respondents such as Abbey and Jessie would view Kosei as one of the privileged, although Kosei herself did not think so. She was more aware of the injustices faced by doctors, who 'work long hours and are misunderstood by the public, fuelled by media prejudices, and have to endure the risk of bodily harm in face of such misunderstandings'. She, too, called for state reform of health care in that she hoped for better management and responsible reporting to improve things from the ground, as expressed below:

> My parents didn't want me to become a doctor because it's hard and it's exhausting and we are treated very badly. The state should reform the system to make sure we are properly compensated for our time, and they should stop the media from printing sensationalist stories when they don't have the medical knowledge to judge what is going on ... there's a breakdown in trust between patients and doctors and that does no one any good.

Lu, who has been in the medical profession for over forty years, has a more rational view towards the matter. He, too, agreed the media is the culprit behind the strained doctor-patient relationship, especially the selective reporting of malpractice cases, even when the evidence is insufficient. He argued that the unequal resource distribution between rural/urban and coastal/inland areas creates a vicious cycle, where tertiary-level first-class hospitals are flooded with patients with minor ailments that could be dealt with easily by local clinics. While the establishment of private hospitals appears to be an obvious answer, Lu also pointed out that private hospitals in China are inherently different from private hospitals in the West.

> We are just starting off, really, that's part of the problem. People trust private hospitals even less, because it costs more. You can't solve it in one or two years, you need time, and an open policy. Allow the capital to go to private health care, and it will allow the current resources distribution to readjust.

The inequality in resource distribution has led to inequality in privilege and access, which is also a major concern for the respondents. They argued that not only is there a rich/poor and urban/rural divide, but there is also great inequality between those who work inside the state sector and enjoy a better benefit package and those who do not. Many of the salaried class in particular were eager to point out that they are also underprivileged, compared to those who work in the civil service and enjoy enormous sociopolitical capital 'beyond [even] what money can buy'. This privilege, they felt, was undeserved, as they do not perceive state sector jobs to have more 'public value' than that in the private sector. Kun reminisced about his parents' time, where 'everyone's contribution to the country was equal and was treated equally', a sense of equity that has since disappeared. Similarly, Jessie described an old lady janitor in her company who had helped to develop Xinjiang for thirty years, before being laid off and now survives on ¥2,000 a month with no state provided healthcare packages, and a civil servant whom she met online, who enjoys an employer-provided housing accumulation fund of ¥200,000 even after an initial withdrawal from the fund. Clearly, she found the stark contrast deeply unfair and she thought the former deserved more state recognition and welfare assistance than the latter.

Nevertheless, although most respondents agreed that they are dissatisfied with the current healthcare situation, they also acknowledged that there is no fast and sure cure for the problem. In fact, quite a few respondents pointed out that no country in the world is completely satisfied with their healthcare system, and China has a 'fundamental disadvantage' of being overpopulated. Their dissatisfaction with the current system has a resigned tone, and does not necessarily translate to a dissatisfaction towards the state. This attitude is significant and also largely congruent with the respondents' attitude in other aspects of life: unhappy, but also holds no real expectations of any major change.

Education: 'Values over profit'

Knowledge is an asset most closely linked with capital and power, two of the most coveted resources in China (Lu 2010). Although research has shown that despite significant sociopolitical upheavals in the last century, China remains a country with high intergenerational privilege transfer and limited social mobility (Clark 2014; Goodman 2014a); one of the few ways to ascend the social ladder is through education. As higher education is one of the defining characteristics of middle classness, there is consensus among the sampled respondents about the importance of education, both as a state provided public good (basic literacy and education should be provided for all), and as a private arena for competition (higher education as a mean to amass greater resources, capital and power). Dissatisfaction with the current state of education is also high (90 per cent mostly or very dissatisfied), and grievances are divided between the value of education and institution of education, both of which are seen as coming under attack from marketisation.

Since the 1990s, China has been continuously expanding higher education, and enrolment numbers have increased from 9.8 million in 1998 to 23.3 million in 2008 (Li, Zhou and Fan 2014). Jane and Ophelia, both of whom attended university during this time, felt that the value of education, especially the cultivation of character, have diminished in the pursuit for profit. Ophelia, who studied Classical Chinese at university, rested her definition of education upon a classical interpretation:

> For me, education is separated into two parts, according to the classical verse. First, teaching is so that students are able to acquire knowledge by following the teacher's example and second, growth can be fostered so that children develop into men of virtues. Regardless of school education or family education, 'teaching' is the most important and teaching always comes from the collective consciousness, what you teach yourself come from others, or what is accepted as the mainstream views. Once you form your own view of the world, the effect of education diminishes.

Similarly, Jane expressed a clear agenda for what educational institutions should be:

> Schools should be somewhere you can settle down, research, teach and mould the next generation, supporting society in offering scientific and technological assistance, all these fundamental things.

Consequently, their dissatisfaction with the current education system is very much a sense of dissatisfaction towards how these educational ideals are actually realised. They complained that education was being monetised in today's society, which is the root of the problem, a view that is shared by many other respondents. Jane described today's society as being 'frivolous': the eagerness for quick success is so pervasive that the point of education – a 'distillation of wisdom, a long-term investment in the future and a quiet place for contemplation' – has been lost. To Jane, China's schooling system faces a fundamental conundrum – that it is state controlled, but operates in a marketised fashion. Research targets, which universities assign to the professors, coupled with the meagre, state-provided wages, drive them to moonlight as tutors and focus too much of their time on reaching allocated 'publication' quotas, instead of teaching. The market, she believed, requires a quick return from investment, and that is fundamentally incompatible with the ideals of a good education. Ophelia voiced a similar concern that in primary and secondary education, schools would set up all kinds of fees under different names to cover the cost of teaching, and parents would have to comply, out of fear that the teacher will discriminate against their children if they do not pay. Whereas the state is supposedly in control of education, it falls short both in funding and support, forcing schools and universities to fill the gap with marketised strategies. In their opinion, this arrangement leaves the current system in an awkward position.

For elderly respondents whose experience of education comes not from their personal memory but from their role as a parent or grandparent, their critique of the current education system is more about the practicalities of school enrolment than its values. The restriction of *hukou,* the household registration system in China, and the steeply priced 'school district housing' are often cited as the main hindrance to a fair education system, as is the discrimination faced by migrant workers. Many were able to appreciate the fact that for them and their children, the access to education is not a problem, since they all have urban *hukou* and have established themselves firmly in cities. They were acutely aware of others who are less fortunate, such as the children of migrant workers, whose most basic education is not guaranteed. For them, the inequality of the system comes in absolute and relative terms: absolute inequality lies in the *access* to education, whereas relative inequality lies in the *quality* of education. To them, the school is but another social battleground, where parents fight over resources to establish the best of futures for their children.

In general terms, the inequality of resource distribution between urban and rural areas was a main point of concern. Not only are good universities concentrated primarily in big cities, but it is well known that students in key urban areas such as Beijing have a much better shot at top universities than their rural counterparts. In 2012, for example, the entrance requirement for Peking University in Beijing was 654/702 points, and 150 students were recruited, while in Hebei, the entrance requirement was 689/700 for the same university, and only 8 students made the cut in the entire province. In further inland rural areas, kids face even more inherent disadvantages: their struggle out of poverty is often met with obstacles such as inadequate teaching resources, unfavourable locales of schools, family pressure (being asked to work at an earlier age) and, curiously, the lack of access to extracurricular tutoring sessions. Indeed, since the respondents of this sample pool are all urban residents, many of them highlighted the fact that in today's education system, a significant part of the 'race' occurs outside the classroom. Without extracurricular tutoring, there could be no competitive edge, and those without a competitive edge are automatically considered as 'losing out'. The practicalities of fighting for better educational resources often comes down to economic position: with money, better housing can be afforded, a life can be made in the city and extracurricular classes can be arranged. The hidden price tag attached to education is in itself indicative of the inequality of the system.

Unlike health care, however, where the majority of the respondents felt a mixed ownership system was desirable, opinion on the privatisation of education was more varied. Some felt the introduction of private schools should be welcomed for the same reason as private hospitals, whereas others argued that it would further emphasise the role of money, and exacerbate the inequality. It is worth noting that private schools in Ningbo (and to an extent in China in general) are typically considered of poorer teaching quality, where the 'entrance requirement is money rather than grades'. The majority of private universities are seen as low performing and are generally not considered as real competitions against top universities. Those who supported the establishment of private schools typically assumed that in a dual-track system, private schools, like private hospitals, would offer better quality education, while the state would act as social security and provide the bare minimum required for the poor (the compulsory nine-year education). Others do not feel this is a given, and worry that the introduction of private schools would simply put money alongside, or above grades, so that there will be even less of a chance for the poor to break out of poverty through education, as expressed below:

> I think privatisation is unadvisable. Stay the way we are right now is okay, but there are too many people in China, any simple move towards privatisation in anything is unadvisable. This is the lesson we learned through Russia's shock therapy. Besides, Chinese people have always valued education, many people see it as a way to change the lives of their children for good. If you privatise that, people not only have to face personal challenges but also external challenges of money and power in their hopes to make something of themselves – though the problem exists even today, just not as exacerbated. Privatise schools, then good schools like provincial key schools need both good grades and money for entrance. What about the poor, then? I think that'd cause even greater class divide, and would cause those bright children who would otherwise have a shot at breaking free from the lower classes lose their chance at social mobility once and for all.
>
> —*Kosei*

In the end, the respondents expressed similar sentiments towards the education system as they did towards health care: that it is not perfect, has many flaws, but there is no easy way to reform it. Indeed, some respondents felt that despite all of its inequalities, the University Entrance Exam is still the fairest thing in China, because it is purely based on merit. The respondents recognised that the factors contributing towards educational inequality are not exclusive to the educational system, per se, and are reflective of inequality in society as a whole. As a result, while they expressed disappointment in the current situation, they also acknowledged that 'reform should be slow and it's like crossing the river while groping the stones'.

Pension: 'Neither here nor there'

From 1995 onwards, China has had a pay-as-you-go approach to pensions, and despite continuous attempt at reform, the state pension system is near the verge of bankruptcy due to an ageing population (Pitsilis, Von Emloh and Wang 2002). Of all the areas that are considered state responsibilities, pension is the only topic that was met with a demoralised attitude, as well as deep dissatisfaction. Approximately 87 per cent of all respondents were unhappy with the current pension setup, which was unaffected by their class identity, age or income. There was low, almost no expectations: the respondents either laughed outright at the notion of an old age provided for by the state, or noted that the pension scheme appears 'great on paper' but 'next to impossible in realisation'.

It is particularly interesting to see how the low levels of expectation drove the respondents to seek alternative arrangements for their future: unlike health care and education, which were seen as public sector affairs and ones over which the individual has very little control, very few respondents demanded the state to take care of them in their old age, and instead worried over their own ability to look after themselves as the state will undoubtedly fall short of the task. Despite discontent with the pension scheme, the lack of expectation on their part also meant there was no real resentment towards the state, and the respondents do not feel it is an area in which the current Chinese state can be expected to perform well. In fact, many acknowledged that the issue of pension is one experienced worldwide, in developed and developing countries, due to an ageing population. Similar to health care and education, they did not expect the state to come up with a simple solution to the problem, and believed it was more practical for them to tackle the problem on their own.

The only source of major resentment in this area is again related to tax. Many respondents explained that they felt the pension scheme was unfair, mostly because the amount they would receive in their old age is disproportionate to the amount they contribute during their working years. Civil servants and their privileged care packages are again outlined as a major example of inequality, a prime example of disproportionate contribution and rewards. However, many respondents also indicated that the rural residents 'have it worse', so that they have no real justification to bemoan their own situation, even though the civil servants are clearly getting unfair privileges. In this context, they also saw themselves as being in the middle, and any acrimony associated with the inequality is offset by the knowledge that they are not in the lowest in the social order. Lu commented flippantly:

> [The pension scheme] is not fair, of course, but rural residents would have it worse. I'm not too worried about my own pension and old age though; I am after all middle class, and I have my own savings. If even I can't survive, how can anyone else? There'd be riots! [laughs]

This need to secure one's own future would, presumably, lead to a high savings rate among the respondents. However, Table 3.3 show that most respondents would divide their income by half, and those who consider themselves middle class would inch towards the spend more side of the scale.

The primary reason for a lack of clear tendency towards saving is, according to the interviewed respondents, a lack of *ability* to save rather than the lack of *desire*. Many explained their worry for the future is rooted in their inability to

Table 3.3 On a scale of 1 (save everything) to 10 (spend everything), how would you categorise your spending habits? (n=258)

	1–2	3–4	5–6	7–8	9–10
Salaried class	4%	18%	54%	20%	5%
Middle class	0%	18%	48%	30%	4%
Overall	2%	18%	51%	25%	5%

save as much as they would like, as their income is spread thin over mortgages, daily expenses, costs of supporting a family and such. While the middle class does appear to be marginally more confident in their financial abilities, hence likely to spend more, they were equally aware of the need for a 'rainy day fund'; thus, their class identification made no real difference regarding their opinion of the pension scheme.

Furthermore, the respondents' low expectations of the state were reflected in, or perhaps because of, their lack of confidence in the long-term stability of their environment. Taking this view did not mean they believed the Chinese state would collapse or become unstable; rather, they believed that the continued effort of the Chinese state to create a stable society will result in a rapid change of policies that they could not possibly foresee. The prospect of a state-provided old age pension was so out of their control that there was no point in even entertaining the notion. This level of cautiousness was reflected in their savings attitude as well: middle class respondents such as Aline explained that she would not place all of her savings in a single currency, or a single bank, and would much rather direct her savings in hard investment such as real estate, which was less likely to collapse. This sense of self-reliance is best illustrated by Kun's comment about public services in general:

> Look, everything you mentioned before, health care, education, pension ... it really doesn't matter to me, in the end. Because what the state offers in terms of welfare is so pitiful that I know I have to rely on myself. I was never naive enough to think the state will look after me in my old age or time of need, that's why I plan everything myself. Of course, if the state can help out, that's good, but I wouldn't count on it. Also, the thing about China is, it changes too quickly. I have 25 years left before I retire, who knows what will happen to the administration before then? Of course, I can't put my eggs in one basket.

Role of the state: 'Freedom within a safety net'

Aside from the selected survey topics, the interviewed respondents were also asked what they thought the role of the state and government *should* be. The reactions to this open-ended line of query were particularly illustrative of how the respondents saw themselves in relation to the state and society as a whole.

The respondents agreed unanimously that the government should be in charge of the public sector, including but not limited to the areas of health care and education, already touched upon in the surveys. However, opinions were more varied regarding how the government should interfere and manage society as a whole, and to what extent.

Many respondents believed that the key role of the state should be to manage society on a macro level. However, the interpretation of what macro-management entails differed from person to person. Public sector and social security were often mentioned together as a key part of the government's responsibility, especially for taking care of the disadvantaged. However, several respondents emphasised that the government should 'handle what the people can't, and not interfere with what the people can handle themselves'. They saw the state as a vessel for the community and the collective good, but not necessarily in possession of better knowledge compared to the individual or the private sector. In particular, the state should be responsible for affairs that were not profitable but necessary – social benefits. Where the people could take care of themselves, they saw no need or desire for the government to interfere. Of course, the significance of this belief lies in the definition of what people can and cannot 'handle', and whether the people, or the state, should be allowed to make such judgements. This discrepancy in the definition regarding what constitutes private and public domains underlines the difference in attitude towards issues of health care and education (public sector affairs), as opposed to pension (self-reliance).

Less ambiguously, many respondents felt that the state should partake in macroeconomic interventions, because it had saved China once from the financial crisis. They were keenly aware of the blow dealt to South Korea and Hong Kong during the East Asian Financial Crisis of 1997, and believed that mainland China 'had it easy' because of the state's active effort at 'cushioning'. However, Wang hastened to add that financial crises were 'special cases' and did not mean the state should intervene under normal circumstances. This sentiment is shared by several others: Kun, Lily and Abbey all argued that the state should only provide 'guidelines', but leave the individual free to move around inside the box. Abbey asserted further that the state should withdraw from private sector competition to allow a fair playing ground, citing that the majority of Fortune 500 companies in China at the moment were SOEs, which she thought was 'not giving the private sector a chance'. The key role for the state, therefore, was to establish reasonable rules and a fair environment, thus 'reducing possible grey areas, and let the market return to the market'. The emphasis was clearly on regulation: they felt the state should supervise the individual, but not dictate his/her behaviour.

Similarly, many respondents emphasised the role of the state in maintaining law and order, and ensuring social stability. The stigma surrounding the notion of *luan* (chaos, 乱) (Qiao and Chen 1994) is still very fresh in their minds and represents exactly what the middle classes wants to avoid: Jessie, Abbey and Lily all expressed concerns about 'the people', whom they saw as naturally disorderly and will descend into anarchy lest some kind of central control was exerted. Again, the sheer size of the Chinese population was cited as a reason for the need to control, as well as its historical legacy, as expressed below:

> To be honest, our society is very complex – you have all kinds of people, the good, the bad and the ugly. The government needs to control that and keep people in line. The key feature of Chinese people is that if no one is managing them, then chaos descends. We've been managed for so long, so used to it, that once that control is taken away, we become chaotic. So, we do need to be managed – to what extent, that's another question.
>
> —Jessie

This sentiment was echoed by Wang, who believed the East is fundamentally different from the West in this matter. Giving the example of how whipping was a legal form of punishment in Singapore, which 'the Americans would not understand', he argued that there were hecklers or 'unreasonable citizens' in China, whose *suzhi* and sense of morality were lacking, and needed a strong hand to keep them in line. Similar to Abbey and Jessie, he believed that this is a historical problem, where 'very little good had been preserved in Chinese culture, compared to the bad'. He explained that self-regulated freedom was a learned habit, giving the example of Iraq, which he believed was unsuited to the American style of democracy, as they were 'used to violence and killing, and solving problems via fists'. The state could not withdraw in these cases, and is even expected to show a stronger hand; otherwise, there would be chaos.

Nevertheless, the respondents did not believe the desire for strong state control over a stable society contradicted with their desire for the state to leave the market alone; in fact, it complemented the idea of a state-provided guideline, a regulated sphere in which people should be allowed to move freely. A 'fair and just' legal system would be a key feature of such a regulated sphere, which many felt China still lacks. Indeed, Kun argued that the market could only be allowed true autonomy in a country with rule of law, which he did not believe was the case for China. He believed China was very much under the rule of men, where 'one did not get things done by following simple protocols, one got things done by contacting the relevant people.' This, he argued, was the epitome of disorder in society, and precisely what the state should seek to regulate, to enable the healthy functioning of the market.

By extension, those respondents who believed the state should regulate society on a macro-level also thought that individual freedoms could and should be sacrificed for the greater good. This finding is consistent with Sonoda's study that suggested the middle class are willing to suppress freedom of speech if they believed it would uphold social stability and help secure their economic freedom (Sonoda 2010). Interestingly, when faced with the hypothetical situation, the respondents typically placed themselves in the role of the 'greater good', rather than the individuals whose freedom was to be sacrificed. Abbey, Jessie and Min all referred to themselves as the 'law-abiding citizens', who have 'nothing to hide', and should be 'the people that the government protect'. They were unworried about the idea of surveillance, citing the belief that all countries with a functional government would participate in similar surveillance programmes. Several respondents, like Lily, believed Snowdon was a traitor. They explained that they were aware of the censorship and surveillance existing in China today, but they have never had confrontational experiences with it; instead, many felt that surveillance, especially security cameras, have made the streets safer and have helped to reduce crime rates. In other words, they felt they were the beneficiaries of state interference; hence, it was logical for them to be supportive of such schemes.

Negotiating the state and the market

Middle class attitudes towards the state and the market are ambiguous at best. On the one hand, they recognise that they are the beneficiaries of market reform, and that the socioeconomic freedom that granted them their middle class position is a trade-off for the pre-reform socioeconomic security; on the other hand, they are alarmed by the lack of regulation in the market and distrustful of 'human greed' that market mechanisms breed. Regardless of whether they think the state *should* guarantee public service, they uniformly agree that only the state *can* improve public service delivery. Private alternatives, while they can be welcomed as a diversification, are in no way replacement for state. Indeed, although dissatisfaction is common among the respondents, the finger of blame is pointed in different directions. This point is significant because the dissatisfaction that comes from the disappointment in the current level of state effort can be very different from the dissatisfaction that stems from relying on the state as a potential remedy for the situation. The former might think the solution lies outside of the current system, while the latter would prefer to work within the system.

Contrary to theses that argue the middle class are the main drivers of privatisation, the respondents of this sample 'mixed ownership' only in the sense of a dual-system where privatised hospitals and schools would exist alongside state-supported ones, to divert and lessen demand on the current system. They believed this arrangement would benefit both the rich and the poor: the rich would no longer monopolise resources and could redirect their capital to receive better quality care, while the poor could secure the most basic of social benefits in a state-provided safety net. However, such dual-systems could never exist without state endorsement. Since both private hospitals and schools can be observed in Chinese society, many believe such a system is already in its infancy and express hope for its continued growth. A moderate difference can be observed between the middle class and salaried class respondents in this matter: slightly more of those who consider themselves middle class were in favour of privatisation, likely because it would mean access to better quality care and education, which they can afford. Their salaried class counterparts, however, were quick to assert the need for the state to improve the current system, which is no doubt more relevant to them. Indeed, any desire they have for privatisation is the desire for the introduction of new private institutions, not the privatisation of existing institutions.

Notably, in this section, quite a few respondents shied away from initially answering, declaring that they 'knew nothing about the government' and did not want to 'pass opinion on something they felt they had no business commenting upon.' When encouraged, however, nearly all of them did have something to say, and many of their opinions were not as under-informed as initially perceived. Their cautious attitude towards all questions of a political nature also suggests that their lack of political participation was not necessary because of apathy, but because of their discretion when it came to discussing topics of such nature. Many, especially the elderly respondents, believed it was not their place to place demands on the state, or have a say in how the state should run their affairs. The idea that they should not supersede their relative positions in the society is both influenced by the Confucian notion of social hierarchy, as well as their experience of state socialism. Indeed, very few respondents mentioned 'rights' when considering the relationship of state and individual, showing that the very concept of rights is still weak.

The respondents' attitude towards the inadequacies in the state pension scheme was particularly indicative of how they had no expectations of the Chinese state in something they thought was an unsolvable problem. Unlike health care and education, where the majority of respondents saw room for improvement, they acknowledged that pension was a universal problem faced by all countries worldwide. Provision in old age was also something the respondents felt they could take care of themselves; thus, there was little disappointment even with widespread dissatisfaction. More curiously, several respondents explained that they felt China changes too rapidly for them to have a blind trust in the system, either by way of a state-provided pension scheme, or a state-supported banking institution. Their attitude was very much 'everyone for themselves', as they saw no viable alternatives in a transitional society. This kind of attitude, coupled with the answers noted above, indicates that this sample pool of respondents typically believed in the power in which the private sector and individuals may be allowed to freely compete.

4 Middle class attitude towards sociopolitical affairs

One of the most central questions to middle class studies in China is its sociopolitical role. In light of China's rapid socioeconomic change following the market reforms, there is contestation over whether the emerging middle class in China will follow the footsteps of their Western counterparts and advocate for democracy due to their increased size, strength, education and ability to participate in public affairs (Lipset 1959; Rueschemeyer, Stephens and Stephens 1992; Mills 2002), or whether they will become supporters of the state like their counterparts in other developing countries, which is largely responsible for shaping their existence (Johnson 1985; Jones and Brown 1994). For the most part, academic opinion on China have veered towards the latter. Studies have shown that despite a universality in rights consciousness among Chinese citizens, the middle class have not translated such consciousness into support for political freedom (Chen and Lu 2011), nor are they willing to engage in active political confrontations despite greater utilisation of informal networks and activities in managing conflict with authorities (Tang 2011). It has also been argued that the middle class, particularly the 'old middle class', are more interested in securing its economic freedom than political freedom; hence, they are supportive of a centralised technocracy (Sonoda 2010). In certain ways, the middle class and the state can be seen to share fundamental interests: promotion of economic growth, protection of private property, maintenance of social stability and restriction of mass political participation, especially of the lower classes (Chen 2002). Yet, little work has been done on the formulation of the middle class sociopolitical outlook, in the context of how they experience, normalise and internalise sociopolitical events around them, and how they arrive at their paradoxical attitudes.

In this chapter, the respondents were asked to consider questions of social inequity and politics from both a conceptual level and in terms of real-life case studies. By highlighting the distinction between their attitude towards generic political concepts, real life sociopolitical events and the actual prospect of sociopolitical reform, we can see that these respondents are particularly adept at differentiating what 'should be', what 'could be' and what 'is'. Due to their education and socioeconomic position, they are typically aware of and accepting of concepts of democracy and social equity; however, they also (believe themselves to) have a sound knowledge of the sociopolitical environment at large, and are aware of the distinction between the desirability of a concept and the feasibility of its implementation. As beneficiaries of the post-1980s reform, the Chinese middle class's expectations of the state, which remain primarily economic, are generally met, which, coupled with their awareness and empathy towards the limits of government, means that expectations towards government accountability and executive capacity among these middle class respondents are largely well managed.

Social justice

According to John Rawls, the concept of social justice can be defined as 'the ability people have to realise their potential in the society where they live' (Rawls 1999). The lack of social justice is usually seen as social inequity (unfairness), which Martin King Whyte had famously argued to be more destructive than social inequality, as it increases people's sense of relative deprivation, and threatens the legitimacy of the current social structure (Whyte 2010). How the middle class fit into this picture is a relatively under-researched subject. On the one hand, the middle class are typically those who have benefited under market reforms; hence, they are likely the keepers of 'rocky stability' (Shambaugh 2000); on the other hand, by virtue of their middleness, they might have a stronger sense of relative deprivation and social inequity, hence contributing to the 'social volcano'.

Table 4.1 shows that for this sample of middle class respondents, there is clearly an acute sense of unfairness in society, which is most pronounced in the areas of income disparity and property ownership. This sense of inequity is relatively dampened in areas of access to employment and education, where a third and two-fifths of the respondents felt was fair, respectively. If these results are

Table 4.1 Fairness in society (n=258)

How fair are the following aspects...	*Salaried class*	*Middle class*	*Overall*
Society overall			31
Income disparity	13	19	15
Ownership of property	11	18	14
Access to education	39	47	42
Access to employment	26	32	31

Table 4.2 Should there be income disparity in society? (n=258)

	Salaried class	*Middle class*	*Overall*
Yes, as a rule	67	73	70
Depends on the situation, but generally acceptable	21	18	20
No, it is unacceptable	4	1	2

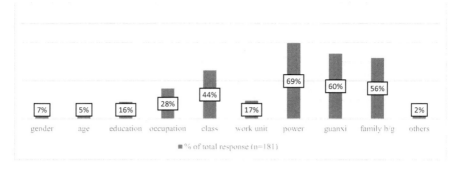

Figure 4.1 Main causal factors behind social inequality and injustice

considered in the context of a typical life journey, then it becomes clear that the respondents thought their chance at a fair competition decreases as they move through stages in their life. While 42 per cent of respondents felt access to education was fair, only 31 per cent felt similarly about employment opportunities, and the number shrinks rapidly when considering gaps in income, and by extension, property ownership. This finding suggests a fundamental mismatch between relatively fair access to institutions that might help to offset social inequality, and their realistic outcome: being granted a fair education and employment opportunities is by no means a guaranteed way to a fair income or property ownership.

Interestingly, however, almost no one thought that income disparity was unreasonable. Despite China's socialist legacy, the results from Table 4.2 show that an overwhelming majority of respondents believed that income disparity should exist in society, in general. This finding is also true across age groups, with small variations: the support for income disparity as a concept is most pronounced in the 40–49 age group, who no doubt bore the brunt of socioeconomic changes during the reform years. Remarkably, the 16–29 age cohort had the lowest support rate of income disparity as a concept out of all age groups, which could be related to their comparatively low starting positions in their career and on the social ladder, and a higher sense of relative deprivation. The 50–70 age cohort, those with memories of the collectivist era, also supported the idea of income disparity in principle, which suggests that little 'socialist' mentality exists.

The top three contenders for the main causal factors behind social inequity are power, *guanxi* (social network and special relationships) and family background, which are undoubtedly interrelated. Although power is seen as the first and foremost casual factor for social inequity, *guanxi* is referred to as the principal component in acquiring power, and the principal form of social capital arising out of a privileged family background. As a result, *guanxi* is nearly always the first response that interviewed respondents jump to when questioned about the reasons behind inequity in society, almost like a knee-jerk reaction in many cases. Aline described the situation as follows:

> Everything can be unfair. If you have *guanxi*, you can do anything. Without guanxi, you get nowhere. That's the biggest factor affecting fairness. Guanxi

undermines legality and legitimacy. Instead of playing by the book, people just take shortcuts. They are always condemning the practice in rhetoric but in reality it's common practice.

The respondents typically referred to nepotism in the workplace and in the admission processes, the nameless and faceless 'leader' and 'boss' who overlooks talent in favour of their kin. While the respondents were able to give examples of casual observations that had occurred in their own workplace, their most vivid imaginations and accusing remarks were directed towards positions of power and key institutions, such as local government, SOEs, and large lucrative private corporations, where jobs are highly desirable but scarce. Whereas the respondents do not seem to discriminate guanxi practice both inside and outside of the public sector, existing research has shown that the effect of guanxi practice is more common in jobs that require 'soft skills', such as newly transformed SOEs, but is mitigated in private sector employment that often has rigorous, 'hard' criteria. Nevertheless, casual observation has reaffirmed their belief that such practice is commonplace, regardless of its intricate reality.

More significant is the respondents' given reason for such 'rife' practices of guanxi. Kosei's answer is illustrative of her criticism for 'institutional' factors behind guanxi culture:

> Mainly I feel people have no moral principles, whereas implicit rules are rife. For example, if you are training to be a doctor and you want a good job at a good hospital, you'd have to give many gifts to the relevant people, or else you'd get nowhere. Education-wise, every single year some of the quota numbers are reserved for children of leaders in the education department, or as a commodity for trade of favours with leaders in other departments. I think it's an institutional problem; people are like water, they are easily influenced by what's outside. If the larger environment is straight, people become principled and morally upstanding – even if they harbour ill intentions, they'd hide it. If the environment is dirty, they'd just do whatever they want.

It is worth noting here that despite pointing the finger of blame at so-called 'institution', it is by no means equated with the regime of government under which China currently operates. Despite being a vague and loaded term, the meaning of 'institution' also appears to be flexible; it is most often referred to without any kind of qualification, and can simultaneously be used to describe China's sociopolitical structure, or culture or historical legacy. What is more significant is that what the respondents *did not* equate it with: no respondents claimed that it was the authoritarian nature of government or the highly centralised style of leadership that was responsible for these grey areas of social practice. Although deemed as amoral and unjust, *guanxi* practice is also at its core reciprocal: one cannot be excluded from it, and one inevitably gains *and* loses in one's participation. Thus, many respondents conveyed a general sense of weary acceptance, using phrases such as 'that's just how it is', and citing 'culture' and 'environment at large' to justify their participation in the practice.

More interestingly, some respondents claimed that to be well versed in guanxi practice in itself is a skill, and hence 'fair' in its own right: either you learn how to play the game, or you lose out. Although they recognise the role their family play in the social capital that is preallocated to them at birth, they also believe that one has to cultivate further guanxi networks oneself to keep on top of the game. In a sense, it is an acquired skill: one needs to learn how to play the game, before he can become proficient. It is also a 'soft' skill that cannot be graded on paper, but at the same time illustrative of one's ability to be a well-functioning member of society, thus is no less – some even argued even more – important.

> The world is unfair, and guanxi is a part of this unfairness – but at the same time, it's fair. Why should a lazy, aloof person be awarded with more guanxi and reap its benefits, than someone who is hardworking and enthusiastic? Talent is something else entirely. Learning how to conduct oneself is even more important than hard work. Those who exclaim society is unfair are the people who didn't get to enjoy the benefits, and it's usually due to the lack of their own effort. Gaining guanxi is a part of personal effort, and a very important one. Being able to work hard is the first step towards success, there are many people who can get things done, but not many who can get guanxi right. That's what separates those who are talented and those who are not.
> —*Abbey*

The participation in this 'culture' of social capital exchange based on human networks, therefore, is in essence a learned behaviour, which could be explained by social reproduction theory. The significance in this is that if people did not view the casual factors behind social injustice to be immoral and condemnable, but simply *amoral* and manipulatable (some people abuse guanxi more than others), then by extension, social injustice is not in itself a grave, non-negotiable offense. If by chance they identify themselves as active participants in the amoral grey practices, then they will have no moral justification to call for an abolition of social injustice at all. Thus, social inequity is not so much a sociopolitical 'problem' but a sociopolitical 'phenomenon', the latter of which denotes a sense of inevitability and immovability. Everyone is to blame here, and no one truly is; no single entity or institution could hope to alter the nature of this grey area, not the government, and certainly not the individual.

Indeed, very few respondents voiced belief in – or indeed desire for – possible change. Many recognised the current leadership's effort at encouraging greater transparency and accountability in the workplace and especially the civil service, but also seemed to think that they are more rhetoric than practice. Yet, their belief in the status quo does not stem solely from apathy but also a deeper, if somewhat subjective, understanding of Chinese society at large: the issue of inequity is often viewed within the historical context of reform, and some were able to acknowledge the checks and balances already in place to negate such effects. Kun commented:

> This unfairness we have runs in generations. Your parents' generation didn't get a head start in the reform era, then you suffer, and so will your kids....

But sometimes I think society is fair. At least you now have a chance to succeed, the opportunities are there, you have the Civil Service Examinations and the University Entrance Examinations. On the other hand, people don't start off on the same foot. If you are rich, you can buy into a better primary school for your kids; if you are not, sometimes your hukou is not even registered in the area, no matter how many years your parents may have worked here. I think we are actually the beneficiaries in the system. My job, my family … by comparison, in China, as a whole, we do quite well. But even I feel it's unfair; so, no doubt some other people who are less fortunate will feel the unfairness more acutely.

Kun may not be alone in his assessment of society becoming fairer for some, despite its increasing inequality. This idea relates back to Martin King Whyte's famous 'equality versus equity' debate, where he outlined that these two terms mean two different things. Indeed, if we input the word 'equality' (*pingdeng*, 平等) and 'equity' (*gongping*, 公平) into Google Ngram, a service used to compute the percentage of usage of a certain phrase that occurs in the corpus of its catalogued books over the selected years, we can observe how the trend of usage for these two words changed over the years. We can see from Figure 4.2 that the usage of 'equality' has been on a more or less steady rise since 1949, whereas the usage of 'equity' only came into focus after the second half of the 1980s Deng's reform. Of course, without context, it is impossible to know how many of these mentions are calls for equity in face of an increasingly unfair society, and how many are mentions of degree of fairness in society itself; yet, it shows that the idea of 'fairness' and 'equity' is relatively new. It is entirely possible that the older cohorts felt society was generally more fair (as aforementioned) because they felt that having unequal opportunities on a wide scale was fairer than having no opportunities at all and that the risks that come with an unfair and rapidly evolving society are actually fair game.

Several respondents were also aware of, and pointed out, the regional differences in the issue of inequity in society. By comparison, they argued, Ningbo does quite well: as an economically well-developed coastal urban region, the local government is not subject to severe resource constraints. Their urban resident status

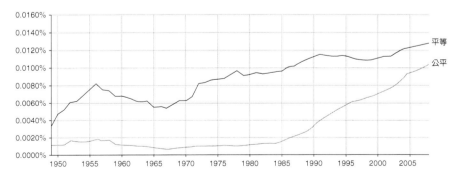

Figure 4.2 Usage of 'equality' and 'equity' over time
Source: Google Ngram

also gives them a significant edge over the sizeable population of rural migrants in the city: being mostly born and bred in Ningbo, they recognise that absolute poverty was never really a concern for them, unlike the population in other poorer, inland areas. Several older respondents also referred to Ningbo people's mild temperament, the 'Confucian merchant's ability to go about [his] own business and adapt to environment at large, however harsh', citing personal observations from the past. Aline described:

> Ningbo is slightly fairer, I think. Because we are a bit cowardly! [laughs]. We are very middlebrow. Look at the Cultural Revolution, some places in China had armed conflicts, violence. Ningbo didn't have that. We were always focused on economic development. If we aren't allowed to develop in one sector for whatever reason, we move on to something else. I'll give you an example. In the 80s and 90s, the export sector in China took a big hit when the SOEs underwent privatisation. So, they've moved all the files [dang'an] of state employees to the human resources market, basically telling you to go look for other jobs. In Beijing, people were panicking because they were being laid off, but in Ningbo, everyone just packed up, and sought another way to make money. We started street-side businesses, went into smaller factories, anything. We thought that was normal, even if the SOEs were supposed to be an iron rice bowl. The people in Ningbo are very well grounded, we take care of our own businesses first, before minding someone else's. I think that's an admirable quality.

As such, they were able to recognise that in a largely unfair environment, they do count among the beneficiaries of reform; thus, any changes would likely hurt their interests. Although a sense of relative deprivation does exist, it is often dampened by the feeling of quid pro quo: many were aware that although they are affected by injustices in society at large, they were both the exploiters and the exploited, but never at the bottom of the pile. Thus, although unfairness is commonplace, conflict is unlikely: less than half of surveyed respondents believed that different classes would come into conflict with each other. Even when they felt conflict was inevitable, it was described as 'between individuals of different classes', rather than classes itself, a result of 'the zero-sum game'. Aside from the obvious grievance against those working within the state sector and civil servants – a recurring theme throughout the study – other areas of conflict were seen as indirect and inevitable, sometimes with the middle class being both the unintended exploiters as well as beneficiaries. Lily explained:

> Class conflict definitely exists. Why can't they pass the pension reforms? Because certain interest groups are blocking it. If the reform is going to harm the interests of the reformers, of course, they are not going to carry it through. Does that count as class conflict? Most conflict you see is between those who work within the state sector and those who work outside of it. Most other class conflicts are indirect. For example, when a lot of middle classes flock into the housing market, the housing prices are pushed up, and that harms the lower classes, who can't afford them. That's unavoidable. Unfairness definitely exists – but can you call it a conflict? It's definitely not worthy of revolt.

Finally, it is worth noting that all of the interviewed respondents acknowledged that a truly fair society can only exist in theory. William joked that there are only two forms of fair society, one is primitive, which '[they] had missed', and one is communist, which '[they] will never reach'. Indeed, the expectation of a fair society is extremely low. This lack of expectation, coupled with the recognition that the current rule of game, though unfair, has granted them a certain amount of gains, suggests that there is little drive to actively and aggressively push for a 'fairer and more just' society among the respondent pool.

Attitude towards democratic concepts

Most studies of middle class political attitudes rely on their attitude towards the *idea* of democracy: whether they subscribe to notions that are generally considered to be integral to a democratic system such as political liberty, participatory norm and competitive election. To better situate the political orientation of this sample of respondents, they too were asked for their opinions on abstract political concepts similar to those found in large national survey samples and studies (Chen and Lu 2011).

The general trend, according to the results in Table 4.3, is clear: when assessed as an objective class category, the respondents of this sample appear considerably liberal in their political attitudes. They are largely supportive of grassroot civil society movements, disinclined to embrace the authoritarian nature of government and are overwhelmingly supportive of multi-candidate and multi-party elections. In several aspects, the middle class respondents of this sample stand out in stark contrast with Chen and Lu's sample of 2011: they are less critical of grassroots movements, and importantly, largely supportive of multi-party elections. Furthermore, unlike analysis from similar questions from the East Asian Barometer (Tang, Woods and Zhao 2009), subjective class identity had little influence on this sample's sociopolitical opinion. On the other hand, rather predictably, Chinese Communist Party (CCP) membership and state employment status did: among the surveyed, more of those who were state employees agreed with the notion that government should be like head of a family (31 per cent as opposed to 13 per cent); and they were similarly more adamant that reform should be led by the government (75 per cent compared to 62 per cent). This result is fairly intuitive as one would expect state employees to have more confidence and reliance in the state itself, as they have vested interests in the existing institutions; indeed, Chen and Lu's somewhat more conservative sample had 60 per cent of state employees, compared to only 32 per cent in this sample, which could contribute to the varying results. Both CCP membership and state employment status have a noticeable influence on the respondents' support for multi-party elections: 62 per cent of CCP members and 66 per cent of state employees favour it in principle, compared to 83 per cent and 82 per cent of their counterparts, respectively. While it suggests a degree of 'towing the party line' for those who are active participants within the one-party state, the fact should not be overlooked that even within the party and state apparatus, more than half would support multi-party elections in principle – which is significant, as competitive elections are a crucial component of a democratic regime.

Table 4.3 Middle class attitudes towards democratic concepts

Statement	% supportive response from Chen and Lu 2011 study	% supportive response in this study	% supportive response from those who think society is fair in this study	% supportive response from those who think society is unfair in this study
The harmony of the community will be disrupted if people form their organisations outside the government.	76.5	26.7	25.6	29.0
Measures to promote political reform should be initiated by the party and government, not by ordinary people (laobaixing) like me.	71.9	60.0	68.4	65.4
Government is like the head of a family; we should all follow their decisions, not our own.	24.9	18.3	22.0	15.5
Political elections should have multiple, diverse candidates.	69.9	88.9	84.2	96.4
Competition among several parties in the election of government leaders should not be allowed.	75.1	20.6	27.8	22.3

Curiously, the respondents' perception of fairness did not appear to have a significant impact on their democratic leanings: the only notable variance appeared under their support for multi-candidate elections, where 96 per cent of those who believed society was unfair gave supportive responses to the statement, while only 84 per cent of those who thought society was fair did. Nevertheless, in either case, the support for multi-candidate elections is overwhelming; what is more significant is that the respondents' perception of fairness did not have an impact on their support for participatory norm or democratic elections. This lack of correlation suggests that people's sense of social injustice does not reflect accordingly with their political attitudes, as they do not equate democratic practices with the alleviation of social unfairness.

At first glance, the middle class respondents in this sample do appear to exhibit what one might call avant-garde democratic ideas. Their overwhelming support for the concept of civil society and multi-party elections is most outstanding: while support for multi-candidate elections is commonplace as it is already in practice in China, the idea of multi-party elections is usually met with caution,

Middle class attitude towards sociopolitical affairs 59

as China is a definitively one-party state, and to support otherwise could be interpreted as a challenge to the current regime. Before we draw the conclusion that the Chinese middle class appear to have matured in their democratic outlook, however, we should pay attention to the idiosyncrasies presented in this sample still: that 60 per cent of the respondents would still prefer reform to be led by the government, despite their otherwise 'democratic' outlooks. This deviation is most significant because it presents itself as a major anomaly; it appears incompatible with the corresponding statement that government is like the head of a family, with which 72 per cent of the respondents in this sample disagreed. As these statements represent opposing sides of preference, it appears the respondents in this sample are at once in favour of authoritarian leadership, and against it. What could have caused such an anomaly? To put these results into context, food safety and the Zhenhai PX incident were presented as case studies of their real-life sociopolitical participation.

Case study: Food safety concerns

Similar to many other areas of Chinese economy, China's food industry took off at breakneck speed after the 1980s, with an annual growth rate of over 13% (Lam *et al.* 2013). Food safety has since become a major public health issue, with microbe contamination, chemical contamination and illegal additives being the primary concerns of legislative bodies as well as consumers. In 2014 alone, there were reportedly 1,480 outbreaks of food-borne illnesses, and 160,000 persons were affected, a 47.9% and 103% increase from 2013, respectively (NHFPC 2014). Contamination of raw materials, insufficient sanitation control and doping of foreign matter into food such as additives and 'eyewinkers' are considered to be primary factors behind these concerns (Bai *et al.* 2007), and it is an issue that is felt keenly by this sample of middle class respondents. Almost none felt food was absolutely safe, and more than half would describe the food in Ningbo to be most unsafe or very unsafe. Among the two self-ascribed classes, a slightly greater proportion of the salaried class appeared to worry or be ambivalent about their food.

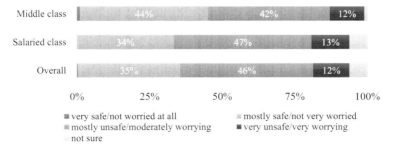

Figure 4.3 In your opinion, how safe is the food in Ningbo?

Aside from a general feeling of concern, there is also a strong sense of government responsibility for the issue of food safety, which indicates the idea of government owing a social duty to its people. This sentiment is largely consistent with the high proportion of agreement in the statement that 'reform should be led by the government', which denotes a high level of expectation for the government to alleviate socioeconomic and sociopolitical problems. First, it is hypothesised that a strong sense of government accountability can increase political expectation, which, if unfulfilled, can in turn fuel radical thinking or encourage grassroot political participation. Second, it appears that a sizeable proportion of the respondents do believe that the ability to afford safe food is directly related to economic well-being, as more than half believe that pricy branded food affords better safety, and approximately two-thirds think that food safety issues threaten the poor more. These beliefs are potentially significant because if people believe that safe food is something only the rich can afford, then it will become a potential source of social conflict. Nevertheless, the overwhelming opposition for the notion that 'food safety is not a problem as long as I can afford safe food' suggests a high sensitivity among the respondents towards social issues, particularly one that is relevant to their everyday lives, regardless of how affected they believe themselves to be. Indeed, the respondents reported a certain level of comfort felt by high earners, combined with a level of empathy for the poor: Kun explained how, despite lurking dangers everywhere, he was fortunate enough to afford some baseline level of assurance, as expressed below:

> I would be somewhat careful when I eat out. If it's a restaurant I don't know, hasn't had any reviews, and it looks dubious, I'd skip it. But I'm not overly concerned. The major concern lies in the rural areas, where the food safety regulations are nonexistent. We have choices in the cities, but not the peasants. I would drink branded milk, and branded water. But once you go into the rural villages, Wahaha becomes knockoff Wahehe and nothing is guaranteed by that.

Furthermore, there appears to be a comparatively strong correlation between the respondents' perception of fairness and their expectation of state responsibility: 95 per cent of those who thought society was unfair believed food safety should be primarily a government responsibility, whereas only 73 per cent of their counterparts did. Furthermore, 71 per cent of those who believe society is unfair think food safety threatens the poor more, compared to just half of those who think society is fair, suggesting that more of the former cohort see food safety as an issue of social inequality as well as inequity. This finding could indicate that perceptions of social fairness could be related to both the respondents' expectation of state responsibilities and their evaluation of state effort; the government is both seen as the cause and the solution to problematic socioeconomic issues.

According to the respondents, the issue of food safety distills down to two major factors: poor governance, and profit-driven moral decay. Most respondents argued that food safety is a major concern in all countries (often citing the horse meat scandal in Europe), but it is the permissiveness of government

Table 4.4 Attitude towards food safety

% of response		Government should take first responsibility for food safety	Pricy and branded food are safer than cheap food	Food safety issues threaten the poor more	It's not a problem as long as I can afford safe food
Overall	Agree	90.6	53.9	66.1	10.0
	Disagree	7.8	40.6	32.8	87.2
% of those who perceive society to be fair	Agree	72.5	52.5	50.0	15.4
	Disagree	27.5	47.5	50.0	84.6
% of those who perceive society to be unfair	Agree	95.1	58.8	71.2	9.2
	Disagree	4.9	41.2	28.8	90.8

legislations that underlines the severity of the issue in China. While food safety assurance systems in terms of quality assurance upon market admittance such as AQSIQ (Food Quality Safety Market Access System) do exist in China, the respondents were more distrustful of their usefulness, and focus on the lack of punitive measures towards violators. They refer to examples of Hong Kong, Japan and Korea, where strictly enforced regulations would discourage any attempt at meddling with food as a means to increase profit. In mainland China, one respondent said flippantly, 'the law is something you plaster on the wall.' Ophelia further argued:

> Food safety is a question of poor governance .... The problem persists because our regulation is lacking. Sometimes the consequence for violating food safety laws is just fines, which people are willing to pay if the profit margin is wider. Or perhaps there are illicit relations between officials and merchants, with mutual interests; then, the merchant will become arrogant in thinking they can do whatever they want. It's no use if there are only watchdogs, but no system of punishment, or if it's not carried out effectively.

More importantly, the respondents traced the root cause of the issue back to 'moral decay', a 'frivolous, anxious mentality' in the pursuit of wider profit margins that drive people to crime. Afterwards, *guanxi* and red envelopes under the table can be used to offset potential penalisation, which further lowers the cost of the crime itself. Kosei quoted a saying that 'a profit margin of 200% will drive someone to risk capital punishment', with which she wholeheartedly agrees: it is because of high profit margins and low risk involved that food safety continues to be an issue. Wang further argued that legislative means alone are not enough to curb these activities, which are driven by greed, one of human's baser desires. Moral upstandingness is what underpins successful governance in this case, as Wang states:

> The government should bear principal responsibility for the ongoing food safety crisis. But that's not all – to maintain a state and a government, morality is

very important. That's why Jiang Zemin advocated 'rule by virtue', because law is not comprehensive enough and cannot cater for everything. Morality or virtue, on the other hand, can fill in the gaps, where the law cannot reach. So, a country should be ruled by virtue as well as law, you need the power of morality to keep people in rein. Nowadays, we've destroyed a lot of virtues, and our moral baseline has been eroded, that's why the crisis of food safety comes up. The law is not all encompassing, what it can do is limited. In order to tackle the problem, we need more self-control, and that's where we are lacking.

Unfair competition and peer pressure are also viewed as a precipitating factor: William advocated the view that if one vendor cuts corners or uses dubious materials in the making of his food and increases his profit margin, it is only a matter of time before his peers follow, since the use of unsafe products is giving him an edge in the business. They subscribe to the idea that this is a question of *suzhi*, and one that can only be offset by education, which again calls for state effort, as William states:

The more pressing concern is to educate people when they are young, better our customs, our *suzhi*, don't let the race for profit tarnish our culture. To think, parents often teach their child 'go and scramble for a seat when you get on the bus!' or tell them it's okay to cross the road when the light is red, as long as there are no cars – these kinds of attitudes need to change, and the state needs to help. Think about it – when everyone else behaves like a wolf, and you behave like a sheep, you get bullied. The state needs to implement some kind of system that protects honest people, who are well educated and actually adhere to societal rules, to make sure that they also gain a foothold in this volatile society, to be able to hold their ground and cultivate interest for themselves.

It is generally agreed that such education needs to 'start young', and it is a common belief that those who are now engaging in this illegal activity are already beyond moral persuasion. Therefore, it was unanimously agreed that heavy penalisations are needed if the present day problem is to be tackled. Increasing the cost of crime also means increasing law enforcement efforts, which circles back to government initiatives. Yamei argued:

If the merchants want to earn their dirty money, then we should fine them so hard that they go bankrupt. Also charge them with criminal liability – once you make the cost of crime extremely high, people will think twice before doing it. We should deal with them like how Singapore deals with drugs.

Thus, by delving into the perpetrating factors and proposed solutions behind the food safety problem, the meaning of the contradictions presented in the previous section emerges. The reason behind strong support for both government-led reforms and participatory norm is that the respondents believed the government should heed the people's appeals and take necessary actions accordingly. The interviewed respondents were reasonably well informed in these issues, and many were able to advocate clearly and strongly about their beliefs. They have certain expectations for the state, but all the while recognising that there are limits to their own power – there is little desire or confidence to take matter into their own hands. In face of institutional defect and moral decay, any individual effort seems futile, as they too recognised the inevitability of someone caving into peer pressure. Food safety, with its myriad of socioeconomic and sociopolitical implications, is simply not a single phenomenon the people could hope to reverse themselves. Instead, the respondents looked towards the state and government as executors of their beliefs, often hoping for a legal implementation of their morals. This kind of attitude is consistent with the Confucian notion of a benevolent but absolute leader; i.e. the government whose power is legitimised by answering to the popular appeal. Indeed, the issue of food safety is peculiar precisely because it cuts across socioeconomic and sociopolitical lines: its motivation is often economic in nature, its impact social and its remedy political. The respondents may be highly vocal about what is wrong and what should be done, but it is always outlined in general, macro-terms, without emphasising the role of the individual, or indeed themselves. Regulation and control, a direct extension of state power, are seen as the only way to rectify these complex problems, as respondents preferred themselves to be passive receivers in the process, rather than active instigators. Therefore, a simple conclusion cannot be drawn between support for participatory norm and decision to participate in democratic processes, or even endorsement of direct democratic processes. The expectation and responsibility for sociopolitical change still rest principally with the government, not the populace as a participatory agent on their own.

Case study: Zhenhai PX incident

From 24 October through 28 October 2012, a series of protests erupted in Ningbo over the proposed expansion of a petrochemical plant to produce the industrial chemical paraxylene (PX) in the district of Zhenhai, a mere 15.5 kilometres away from the city centre. Paraxylene is believed to have severe adverse effects on health, and associated projects have been highly controversial nationwide. Other PX-related projects have been rejected in the cities of Dalian and Xiamen, due to similar protests over health and environmental risks. Emotional pleas and propaganda filled the Internet for weeks leading up to the protest, peaking on the weekend of 27–28 October. The following day, on 29 October, the Ningbo Municipal Government conceded and announced that the project would be halted indefinitely, pending further review.

Although the media (especially the foreign media) were eager to portray this incident, like its counterparts in Dalian and Xiamen, as a "middle-class uprising" (French 2006; Larson 2012), *China Daily* stated that the protests were not inherently a rebellion against the government or even the project, but that the main grievance arose from a lack of information about the project and government accountability for it (Yang 2012). Nevertheless, engaging in such an event of mass mobilisation, as well as being in direct conflict with the authorities, are inherently political, thus enquiring into the nature of and participation in the PX incident is very telling of how the respondents approached real-life sociopolitical events.

According to the survey, overall awareness of the incident was quite high: 65 per cent of all surveyed participants were interested in it. However, actual participation was very low: only 25 per cent participated online and a mere 6 per cent turned up at a protest or participated in some way offline. This result is consistent with previous survey findings that suggest that the middle class have high civic awareness, but low civic association (Wang 2008). No significant correlation was found between the respondents' age, subjective class identity, and their participation. CCP membership and state employment status had a predictable effect on the respondents' participation: those who had closer ties with the state apparatus were less likely to participate in such politically sensitive events. When examined against their answers to the previous question set on abstract political concepts, it appears that the respondents' proclaimed political attitudes did have a degree of influence on their political behaviour, though not tremendously: a larger proportion of those who believed civil society to be disruptive felt disinterested in the PX incident as a whole, while those who saw the government as being like the 'head of a family' were generally more disinclined to get involved, whether through discussion or online participation, by a margin of 15 per cent (see Appendix). More interestingly, those who believed that the government should lead reforms were more likely to participate online, but steered away from offline protest, while those who did not believe the government had to lead reforms engaged in more offline activities. This finding suggests that those who believed in state-led reform initiatives saw online participation both as being a legitimate outlet for their concerns and as being within the purview of the state, as the Internet is censored and monitored. Offline participation, by contrast, was seen to be an extra-state activity, and was thus less condoned by those who believe that the state has an essential role to play in the political process. Of course, the numbers of people who turned up at the protests were nevertheless low. Due to the overwhelming support for multi-candidate elections, the high standard deviation presented for the statement 'I participated online in the PX incident' is more of an outlier because of the small sample size, rather than any strong correlation.

What is more revealing is how the respondents remembered and explained the PX incident using their own rationale. None of the interviewed respondents believed that the incident was an exclusively middle class affair or that the middle class had played a prominent role in the events. Instead, it was typically argued that the motivation behind participation was that 'a line had been crossed', because PX, thought to be highly toxic, was seen as 'threatening people's lives, regardless of class.' Aline, who was not in Ningbo at the time, expressed strong support for

Table 4.5 Involvement in PX incident

	Civil society	Government as head of family	State should lead reform	Multi-candidate elections	Multi-party elections
I was not interested in the PX incident at all.	**3.3**	2.7	0.7	6.5	2.5
I was aware of the incident but not interested in it.	**2.1**	1.9	**3.9**	5.6	3.3
I was both aware and interested in the incident.	1.1	1.3	**3.9**	0.9	**6.0**
I participated online in the PX incident.	0.1	**5.2**	2.1	**21.5**	**6.6**
I participated offline in the PX incident.	0.1	**3.9**	**4.2**	4.0	3.8
Threshold*	2.0	3.8	3.7	11.7	5.4

*Standard deviation of how much each statement on political attitude affects statement on involvement in the PX incident. Numbers greater than the threshold (in bold) denote a strong correlation.

the demonstrations, and stressed that the non-violent nature of the protest was very important, in the following manner:

> I think the Ningbo people behaved very admirably. We protested by silence, we had no violence. It's just the government really didn't like that, either. If I were in Ningbo, I would definitely have joined. It's to do with where we live! If we had nowhere safe to live, then everything else is a moot point. It's mostly young people who took part though, from what I saw. I don't think it's anything to do with classes, it's just a fundamental line that has been crossed, and people will not tolerate that.

Often, the struggle was described as one between those who had a vested interest in the establishment of the chemical plant, and those who had a vested interest in the safety and health of the local area. Some even thought the middle class would be the least relevant party, since they are able to migrate and it is the poor who are most vulnerable against the polluted environment. Lily argued that if it were not for the fact that public health were at stake, people would never have taken to the streets, as shown below:

> I think [the PX Incident] has got nothing to do with the middle class! The middle class will move out of the pollution zone when they can, they won't care. It's mostly the young, and people who have nowhere else to go and have no other options. If their lives are threatened, then they have no choice. If a choice exists, then the Chinese will not take such extreme measures, like go to the streets.

66 *Middle class attitude towards sociopolitical affairs*

Some respondents who are CCP members recalled how they received notice that they may not participate in the protests through their employers, including major cooperations and government institutions. The message was distributed through mass texts and department bulletins, which caused them to realise 'how serious it was'. Jessie recalled the following:

> I posted online saying that I want to go join the protests, and a friend of mine who works at the police bureau privately messaged me and told me not to go. Clearly it was serious – so I listened.

Fear was a major factor in the interviewees' decision to not participate in the protests. Such fear is both underlined by imagined retributions (the 'what if' mentality), and from personal observations of any political persecutions that have occurred with friends and distant acquaintances. Abbey's view on the event was very typical of someone her age and subjective class: although she demonstrated a reasonably good understanding of popular political topics, she preferred to keep her activities in the private sphere, and was reluctant to be actively involved in the public and the political, as shown below:

> I saw the PX incident on the news. Didn't get involved, cos I was busy at home [laughs]. Besides, I'm having a normal routine life, if I get involved – what if they round me up afterwards? I can't risk that. If they want to arrest you, then they will! We are supposedly allowed to go on demonstrations, but in reality we can't.

Lily had a similarly passive response. Although she argued previously that she understood the reason people took to the streets was because 'their lives were threatened', she clearly did not feel it would affect her as much. Contrary to some of the younger respondents, who are more active online, she did not feel the PX incident to be a major political issue, and felt there was very little that she could achieve even if she did participate in it, as she expressed below:

> I didn't get involved. The transparency of the whole affair is questionable at best, by the time I heard, the fuss was almost over. It's not like they posted a notice all over town or something. Besides, I had a friend who was arrested over protests against a power station being built somewhere. The project went ahead, and he got arrested. What's the point?

During the interviews, it became clear that the interviewees had various different rationales to explain other peoples' 'active' behaviour and their own 'passive' stance. Several respondents further identified the root of the problem as a lack of information dissemination and transparency about the PX plant, but did not feel the protest had legitimate environmental grounds. They expressed compassion and understanding of the protesters' cause, but were able to analyse the issue beyond the superficial call to rally. Some respondents believed that the protesters had been misled, not in terms of the outcome of the protest, but in terms of the reasons for participating in the protests. Kun argued that media exposure had put an unfortunate spotlight on PX, while many other more polluting chemical projects were being left unexamined. Although the sentiments and motivation behind the PX demonstrations were generally endorsed by the respondents, they made a distinction between 'understanding' and 'participating'. Many indicated that they personally would not have followed the protesters to the demonstrations, as they felt the risks of participation outweighed the benefits. Lu's distanced, analytical, and somewhat sceptical take on the events is quite illustrative of this train of logic, as described below:

> I have engineer friends who told me that a lot of the chemical factories already established in the area actually emit much more pollution and pose much larger health risk to the residents compared to PX. But as with everything nowadays, there is an ulterior motive behind these movements. Some of the real estate holders stirred up trouble and helped to organise the protest when they found out the project was going to be introduced, which would crash the housing market surrounding the area. So, it really has nothing to do with the middle class. Most of the people who were involved with it were in it to protect their own interests. For me personally, it's a bit far from my life, so I didn't pay much attention to it. I wouldn't give speeches or attend protests myself.

It was clear that these respondents could readily acknowledge and accept the popular rationale behind the protests, but they also prided themselves in 'being able to see beyond it'. As PX is believed to have adverse health effects, they could see that the public's reaction was to be expected; however, because they believed that the adverse health effects of PX had been greatly exaggerated, many respondents felt the cause for protest had been sensationalised and they, therefore, saw the project as less of a threat than did the active protest participants. Instead, because they saw the struggle between industrial and commercial interests over this project, they wanted to disassociate themselves from anyone who appeared 'rash' or 'hot-headed', as they felt that these individuals were prone to manipulation. Even though these middle-class respondents understood that protesters felt that 'a line had been crossed', for them, that line was still at some safe distance. Therefore, the costs of participating in this highly politically charged protest would outweigh the benefits. Nevertheless, the fact that they could sympathise with the protesters suggests that if, one day, that invisible line were to be crossed, then they too might join others in open protest.

Middle class and social stability

Finally, in order to give more context to the results gathered above, the respondents were asked to assess China's current level of social stability and their own opinions on the role the middle class play in maintaining or affecting such stability.

Due to their sensitive nature, these questions could not be included in the larger questionnaire survey, but instead were asked exclusively in the more intimate setting of interviews.

When asked to evaluate China's present level of social stability, most respondents placed their assessment on the stable side of the scale – that is, they generally allocated a score from 6 to 8, where 1 denotes complete instability and 10 represents total stability. It was unanimously agreed that Ningbo is more stable than China as a whole, and the respondents gave the city a score of at least 8 or 9 on the stability scale. The mild temperament of local residents and their propensity for undertaking money-making activities rather than expressing political ambitions, together with the prosperity of the region and its lack of natural disasters, were the primary reasons for the respondents' high levels of confidence in Ningbo's stability, both at the present and in the long term. Of course, it is likely that, as they also belong to the population of Ningbo, these respondents might also ascribe similar favourable characteristics to themselves and also might subscribe to the same rationale for their own reticence towards political participation and reform.

Several respondents pointed out that social stability is also a subjective experience, hence relative. They believed that the elite classes – defined as 'the people with power and control over key institutions (such as the government) in society' – would view society to be more unstable than '*laobaixing*' like themselves, because the elites have 'more to lose' in the event of social upheaval. The current push for reform, together with the policy of 'tighter security without showing', is seen as a testimony to the keen awareness of potential social unrest at the leadership level:

> On a scale of one to ten as a content member of the middle class, I'd think China's current social stability stands somewhere on an eight. But from a bottom class' point of view, it could be a two or three, and the upper class may see it as a six – as a member of the leading elites, he must have seen the need for reform, hence all the new measures. The middle class gets off the easiest.
> —Jane

The respondents also had varying definitions of stability: for some, stability is underlined by law and order, without 'disrupting incidents', be it petty theft or mass protests. For others, simply internal peace and a lack of open warfare are enough. Regardless of definition, however, all of the respondents stressed that Chinese society will not face any immediate breakdown. Although agents of instability do exist, they argued, it will not amount to real instability, because people are still issue-oriented, and any momentum for fundamental change automatically disbands when the original grievance is addressed.

Generally, the respondents believed that the middle class would be stabilisers of society, rather than agents of change. This belief is partly due to the casual observation of Western middle class societies, and partly from their own experience. Those who could remember a time of poverty often made vertical comparisons with their past, arguing that they were the beneficiaries of society's change, thus would not endanger the very sociopolitical system that brought about those benefits. The younger respondents were similarly aware of the benefits that a state sector job would bring – one respondent related a story where his most 'rebellious' friend, who often spoke against the state, joined the civil service at the first opportunity upon graduation. Thus, many respondents expressed a certainty that the middle class will not be partial to extensive and uprooting reforms, due to their high living standards, and the state policies that aim to promote these lifestyles. Concurring with the present day 'middle class society' narrative, they agree that the middle class would have a vested interest in the status quo, since they are the 'haves' of present-day society.

> As the saying goes, those barefoot are not afraid of those with shoes, if everyone is poor, then society is bound to be unstable. That's the way people think – only when you are in possession of something that you care, that you have reservations. The more you have, the more caution you will have. When you have nothing, you aren't afraid to kick up a fuss.
>
> —*Jane*

Change, in this case, is seen as volatile and unpredictable – it could work in their favour, but it could also damage their interests. Curiously, several respondents made references to migrant workers, whom they believe would be the most unstable group in society, as they experience the highest levels of relative deprivation, and are undergoing the most extensive socioeconomic changes. The middle classes, or even the self-identified salaried class with a steady income, were seen as the least unstable, simply because of the stability in their own lives.

None of the respondents subscribed to the idea of a 'middle-class awakening', whereby the middle class would develop political demands on top of their socioeconomic stability; instead, they argued that any motivation for change would come from defensive desperation, rather than proactive demands. The phrase 'If you are poor you will think about change' came up frequently during discussions, bringing to mind William Cobbett's famous quote, 'You cannot agitate a man on a full stomach'.

> Being middle class means being well educated and with better *suzhi*, which means they will not opt for anything violent or sudden, instead going for gentle reform. Only when reform is proven ineffectual, or the option of reform is taken away, that the middle class will go for revolution … Sun Zhongshan (Sun Yatsen) was middle class too. He wrote to Li Hongzhang in the hopes of prompting government reform and got beaten! So, he had no choice but to start a revolution. It's practically forced out of him. All revolution started with reform – it's only when people see reform being impossible that they resort to more drastic means.
>
> —*Jane*

By contrast, many respondents praised China's current efforts at reform and said that they believed these efforts would appease the minority within the middle or lower middle classes who are not entirely happy with the status quo. If not, they joked, the middle classes can always 'vote with their feet', and emigrate to another country, where their political demands would be better met. Open calls for reform were seen as confrontational and the 'worst strategy possible', since they would most likely prompt an adverse reaction from the state. The respondents' overall confidence in state-led reforms was reasonably high. The respondents did not typically see the state as oppressive or autocratic. They emphasised that the leadership also sought stability and would allow for necessary reforms to maintain stability. Thus, it could be said that the respondents' goals and interests were aligned with the state, which they saw as a leader, as well as an ally, rather than an opponent. Indeed, the current leadership's propensity for reform appears to boost the respondents' confidence in China's long-term stability, as expressed below:

> I don't think there will be any major instability and changes in China. When I was younger, I thought there was a good chance of sociopolitical turbulence, but now I don't think so anymore. Especially with the new leadership, they are all talking about reform, and I think that's great. Once you reform, you avoid the chances of a major upheaval. I think the new leadership knows this and this is their subtle way of saying, we need to change.
>
> —*William*

By extension, Aline warned that if the state undermines middle class interests or if the middle class believe that the state is undermining their interests, then this mutually beneficial partnership might fall apart. The shrinking and devaluing of the stock market and financial products, together with skyrocketing prices in the housing market, argued some, are already putting pressure on the middle classes. With their savings devaluing in the banks and real estate becoming increasingly unaffordable, the very basis of the middle class – income and property, in the eyes of many – is threatened, along with the prospects for stability. Nevertheless, the same respondents hastened to add that they themselves would not hope for instability or change, since it is always the *lao baixing* – 'ordinary people', which is an overarching term that the respondents primarily identified with, rather than referring to their class – who lose out in times of flux.

Indeed, although some respondents were wary of the possibility of instability if the collective interests of the middle class are undermined, none of the interviewed respondents believed they would be an instigator of reform. The respondents' personal attitudes towards sociopolitical change are, in fact, very reserved. The younger respondents exhibited the same 'passive acceptance' that was seen in previous topics that dealt with social injustices and institutional inadequacies – claiming that they are aware that the status quo is not perfect, but there is very little that can ostensibly change. Their search for 'better alternatives' so far comes up empty, and any prospect of sociopolitical change is riddled with risks and unpredictable outcomes, whether imagined or real. One respondent drew a particularly vivid image, as expressed below:

> To go for reform now is like standing in a dark room with no light. Now you might be told there is a light somewhere in the room, but there are a hundred switches and only one of them is real, the rest electrocutes you. Else the room is filled with swords and daggers, and every step you take is filled with traps. How do you propose you move then? Of course you stay in the dark, and stay where you are.
>
> —*Weisheng*

Furthermore, many of the younger respondents also expressed concern that they do not feel they belong to any group of significance, or indeed class, that could act as a coherent political entity. They explained that while they are content to label people of similar socioeconomic background to them as 'middle class', this does not hold any behavioural significance, as expressed below:

> When I look around, I see people similar to me, in terms of living conditions and other habits, and I might label them middle class, too. But I cannot imagine sharing a same political goal – or any goal – with them, for wanting the same thing, or anything significant enough that I would work alongside them according to this notion of class.
>
> —*Jinying*

Whereas the younger respondents were particularly quick to disassociate themselves from 'class consciousness' of any kind that might have a sociopolitical impact, the middle-aged respondents highlighted their preference for focusing on their private lives, thus making them disinclined towards change. A distinction was made frequently between those people who 'keep their heads down' and 'go about their own lives', a group of people with whom many of those interviewed identified, and the 'angry youth' (*fenqing*, 愤青), the '50-cent army' (*wumao* 五毛: a slang term for Internet commentators hired by the state to post favourable comments about party policy, so-called for the 50 fen (0.5 CNY) they allegedly receive for each post), and the 'American saboteurs' (美分, *meifen*: a slang term for Chinese netizens who 'worship' the United States and are overly critical of China) who are active primarily on the Internet. The former group was seen as rational, calm, and unswayed by sensational headlines. They were also seen as not necessarily apathetic, but better informed. The latter were instead criticised for being rash and eager and for 'rushing to the forefront of public attention whenever injustice arises', thus being prone to manipulation.

The older respondents saw the notions of reform and stability through the lens of their own life experiences. For them, the terms 'political participation' and 'reform' resonated with specific, historical meaning, which led them to believe that a recurrence of these themes was not possible, or indeed desirable, anytime soon. Even though the phrase introduced alongside the term 'political participation' in the discussion was 'reform' (*gaige*, 改革), many elderly respondents substituted this phrase with the words for 'revolution' (*geming*, 革命), a term which they then used interchangeably with 'reform'. This kind of mixed usage suggests that the older respondents' idea of active political participation was a more radical and violent one, echoing the events of their childhood. This negative connotation was likely to discourage them further from supporting any future calls for reform. Junhui's answer was perhaps most illustrative:

> The idea is, first you have a revolution for yourself, where you improve your own lives, then you develop a revolutionary consciousness and try to improve the lives of others. The problem is, once you better yourself, you tend to stop, because you are happy now. So, I don't think there are any drastic reforms or revolution coming, because there is no point.

Meanwhile, a small number of respondents exhibited a certain level of pragmatism vis-à-vis the idea of proactive reform. They stressed that they would not initiate any demands for reform or change, but would evaluate any opportunities for reform should they arise. They said that action was warranted only if the timing, need, and leadership were right, in accordance with the Chinese saying 'opportune time, advantageous terrain, and popular support'; therefore, action was not required if the situation was "just a fussy scandal of no consequence." Far from being the initiators of reform and active pursuers of change, these middle class respondents preferred to take the role of watchful bystanders, lest their actions destabilise the status quo, as described below:

> People like us … I think we are the ones seeking change amid stability. We want change, but we won't actively do something about it. Not unless change comes first. If the opportunity arises, of course, I will grasp it.
>
> —*Min*

Together with their acute awareness of the existing opportunities and pitfalls in the current economic climate and the acknowledgement of their relative success under such a climate, the respondents' tentative attitude towards change and their hope for continued betterment are perhaps best illustrated by one respondent's reference to the famous opening line of *A Tale of Two Cities*, an epic story also set in a time of great transformation:

> People like me, I wouldn't want instability, that'd be good for no one. Honestly, I think it's like Dickens said, 'It was the best of times, it was the worst of times.'. Right now, we can really make something for ourselves if we try, the opportunities are there. But society is evolving so fast, if you can't grasp the opportunities or jump on the wrong wagon, you'd end up being miserable. I don't like change. If you look at the films and TV shows depicting great eras of change, they are all bloody and turbulent.
>
> —*Kun*

Understanding the paternalistic state

This chapter considered the respondents' sense of social injustice, their political orientation and their willingness to participate in sociopolitical affairs. Both the survey and interview data suggest that there is an overwhelming sense of unfairness associated with the current sociopolitical structure, which is most pronounced in the aspect of income disparity and property ownership. The respondents drew upon a variety of factors that they thought were incremental to the inequality and inequity in society, from 'cultural constraints' such as amoral guanxi practices to institutional barriers such as the detriment of *hukou* to educational access and the privileges enjoyed by civil servants to income disparity. This acute sense of social injustice is particularly significant because, as Martin King Whyte highlights, there is a distinct difference between the sense of 'equality' and 'equity' in society, with the latter having a more socially destructive impact (Whyte 2010). Unfairness is what underlines the lack of equity, along with the sense of relative deprivation. Studies have shown that sense of justice and equity in social policy is most important in relation to subject's happiness, that a high sense of injustice leads to greater discontent (Mok, Wong and Zhang 2009; Sun and Xiao 2012). Does this mean, then, that dissatisfaction stemming from an acute sense of inequity will lead to instability in the case of the Chinese middle class?

Such a conclusion cannot be drawn so hastily. Although both survey and interview data suggest a heightened sense of inequity in society, a detailed interview analysis reveals that the respondents have a very low expectation or desire for change. In accordance with studies that claim middle class have 'vested interests' in the state and represent the current status quo, it would seem that the respondents in this study are aware of the fact that their very position in the middle of society means they are the beneficiaries of the current system. While they do not necessarily call themselves 'haves', they acknowledge that they are not 'have-nots' either – being in the middle means they stand to gain in the game, even if it means occasionally they also lose out. Any reshuffling of the cards might compromise what they have already learnt and gained in the game, thus undesirable at this point. Again, this finding highlights the need to reconsider the assumed translation between attitude (keen awareness of injustice) and behaviour (resulting in change or instability). Without a desire for difference – or what one might call a 'catalyst' – the recognition and acknowledgement of inequity may not necessarily result in behavioural changes.

Correspondingly, the results from this chapter reveal a divergency in the respondents' political orientation and their tendency towards political participation. On the one hand, when asked in general terms and regarding events of an overtly political nature, the middle class showed strong support for political liberty, competitive elections and participatory norm, all aspects that might point to the 'democratisation of the middle class'. On the other hand, when specific case topics were introduced, the level of proactive participation was very low, and actual participation onsite was almost negligible. Nonetheless, this lack of hands-on approach does not mean that the middle class are in reality politically apathetic, quite the contrary: they appear reasonably well informed about sociopolitical issues that affect their daily lives, and are able to give detailed opinions on where they think the problem lies and what they think can be done about it. They are, however, extremely hesitant towards the idea of taking political action; the consensus remains that any reform or political change needs to come from the state. In accordance with the Chinese saying "let him who tied the bell on the tiger take it off", it is believed that the main causal factors behind major sociopolitical issues are also the main agents needed for change. Not only is the effort of the state required in order to remove the institutional barriers and cultural constraints causing the problem, but the government and the people have to work in tandem, and individual action is seen as purposeless and unhelpful. Many respondents exhibited a sense of sympathetic understanding by acknowledging the practical difficulties of tackling any sociopolitical issue, and differentiated themselves from those who do take political action, whom they see as rash, emotionalised, under-informed, and even easily manipulated.

Thus, to put Whyte's argument in a wider perspective, an awareness of inequity alone does not necessarily lead to anger and dissent. Resentment comes from expectation – without expectation, disappointment and resentment become muted. While it is generally accepted that China's party-state, due to its lack of effective democracy, holds no accountability to the public, the more important question to ask is: 'does the Chinese public expect accountability from the government?' The answer is neither simple nor straightforward. The social contract between the individual and the government is not the same in China as it is in other established democratic countries; it has undergone dramatic change from the socialist era to the post-reform present day. As Tang and Parish have pointed out, the social contract under Mao was that basic living needs were met in return for political acquiescence, whereas under reform, greater individual freedom had been granted in return for less social security, greater risks and competition (Tang and Parish 2000). The transition and negotiation of balance between the individual and the state are almost contrary to the development trajectory of the West, where classical Liberal ideas of 'leaving the drunkard in the gutter' came before the welfare state. By vertical comparison, the responsibility of the state has retreated in China whereas it has expanded elsewhere, such as in Britain. This change inevitably has an impact on people's expectations of what the government should and should not be held accountable for, which is more complex than the simple observation of whether government accountability exists.

Furthermore, differences should be drawn between people's theoretical expectation of government responsibility, and their assumption over the pragmatic realisation of such responsibility. While the middle class might assert that the government holds responsibility over areas of sociopolitical concern, how they expect these concerns to be dealt with and whether they think these concerns can be dealt with at all are more important. In areas where the call for government accountability is high, expectation of accountability is almost always related to, if not equal to, expectation of government-led change. In other words, the middle class do recognise the government's ineffectiveness in certain areas, but they also strongly believe that only the government could be the leading instigators of change. Inversely, when they assume that an issue is so complex that the government could not settle it to universal satisfaction within pragmatic limits, such as the rising income disparity or pension, the expectation of government action or indeed any structural change is correspondingly low. This take on government accountability – and actionability – leads to a wildly different conclusion than, say, if the middle class believed the government is being ineffectual; hence, the solution to their problems should be sought elsewhere. The overwhelming support for the state, rather than the individual or civil society, as the leading instrument for change, thus signifies that grassroot instigated sociopolitical instability is unlikely.

The reason behind this line of thinking could be largely historical. China's unique development trajectory, from socialist to market transitions within several generations, no doubt plays a role in people's perceptions of the role of the state, and their idea of social justice and an egalitarian reality, coloured by memory. Yet, it is possible that such expectations and support of the state could be traced much further back. The Confucian tradition that encourages individuals to perform his or her role within a given social hierarchy could explain why the idea of rights is still weak even among the middle class, who, in this study, have exhibited that they have retained Confucian values at the same time as embracing Western enlightenment ideas. Furthermore, the idea of people-based governance, dating back to Mencius, has always placed the legitimacy of the Chinese state in its ability to satisfy the people's needs. Historically, the people had no input in this process, so that it is a trust-based relationship that the people grant the state legitimacy if they feel the state is making decisions beneficial to them. Indeed, if the state fails to meet the people's expectations, it is seen to have lost the Mandate of Heaven, hence legitimising dissent. Again, the key aspect of the relationship – a social 'gentleman's agreement' instead of a contract (Ling and Shih 1998) – is the people's expectation of the state, which is not the same as people asserting their lawful rights and demanding a return for any rights that they may sacrifice.

In line with the Confucian tradition, the state is viewed as paternalistic, where loyalty towards, and expectations of, the state are similar to the idea of filial piety. To stretch the analogy further, in a child's growth, there inevitably comes a time when the father figure is demystified and no longer appears omnipotent or indeed omniscient. Yet, growth also comes with knowledge and awareness, so that disillusion eventually turns into understanding: a certain empathy towards the father figure, who must also face pragmatic and practical constraints bound by its own limitations. For the middle class, they appear empathetic enough that they realise that the state cannot be held accountable for every social injustice that they might observe or experience, and if any real, practical change was to be made, the state must play a key and leading role in it. Since the state's legitimacy comes from being able to meet the people's expectations, unless those expectations far exceed the capacity of the state to fulfil them, there is no legitimacy in dissent; hence, regime instability is unlikely.

Coming back to the primary debate on middle class political participation, which is whether they will fulfil the role of a stabiliser in society, or agents of change, it seems that either of these terms is too proactive. The middle class respondents in this sample are better labelled as 'passive observers', watchful at best, but extremely cautious towards instigating change. Indeed, with the knowledge that they have on the current system, the Chinese middle class are largely disinclined towards changing the status quo. This conclusion, however, is not as simple as stating that the middle class are conservative in their political outlook. It appears that they do not hold a positive or negative view towards the status quo, but rather see it 'as it is'. For them, it is most important that they understand the system, and play well in it. In a sense, they are the beneficiaries of the system, so that they are unwilling to change the rules or reshuffle society in a way that might harm their interests.

More importantly, there is no evidence that the middle class view themselves as a separate political entity, one that is on equal or similar terms with the state. Their support for democratic notions is within the complex set of expectations they have for the state, and it should be analysed within those contexts. Indeed, the results from this chapter have shown that their relationship to the state – i.e. they are members of the party and work within the state apparatus – is more important than their subjective class identity in determining their political attitude. There is no desire or indeed need for the middle class to take proactive action, as they do not (some might argue dare not) situate themselves opposite the state. However, neither will they necessarily always position themselves alongside the state. It might be presumptuous to assume that the middle class by definition will support the state because of their vested interests, because their expectations may very well change. The vested interests of the middle class in the state are largely economic, as they are the beneficiaries of socioeconomic reforms in the last few decades. Their realistic political expectation in the form of participatory norm is very low – they might agree to it in principle, but hold no expectation of complete political reform overnight, or indeed any political reform that occurs outside the purview of the state. Hence, the paradox in their belief and behaviour: liberal in attitude surveys, conservative in political action. In a sense, the state has met their expectations, and the legitimacy of the current socioeconomic order can be established. Should those expectations evolve, the state must adapt in order to respond to them. So far, the move of the new leadership is deemed as promising: in tightening the controls on the bloated civil bureaucracy, it has begun to address one of the key issues of inequity in society, which is met with approval. Yet, to address one side of injustice is inevitably to harm certain vested interest groups – how the state chooses to balance these expectations could be instrumental in ensuring future regime stability.

5 Nationalism among the middle class

The question of China's rising nationalism is at the forefront of China watchers' mind worldwide. The extent of Chinese nationalism and its potential influence on China's foreign policy is closely related to how other countries – particularly America – view China in the context of her rise to become the world's next superpower. In a policy report drawn by the CATO Institute in Washington, analysts outlined two camps of dividing opinion on how China is perceived, and how America should react to the rise of China – the optimists of 'panda huggers', on the one hand, and the pessimists of 'dragon slayers', on the other hand (Logan 2013). They fundamentally disagree over the impact of China's economic growth on its foreign policy and security goals: the optimists usually turn towards modernisation theory and democratic peace theory to argue that continued economic growth will foster a strong middle class, which will in turn help the establishment of a democracy, and we will gain peace because war between two democratic states is unlikely. The pessimists believe China will eventually assert its economic and military supremacy to expand, which will inevitably come into conflict with today's existing world powers.

In contrast to the development of modern nationalism elsewhere, which often emerges out of the struggle of a modern nation-state against an empire, Chinese nationalism in the 20th century rose as a response to foreign aggression, and the disillusionment of Confucian culturalism (which, paradoxically, has experienced a revival since the 21st century). This historical sense of 'national humiliation', still widely present in public discourse today, is juxtaposed against the CCP's revolutionary and anti-imperialist legacy as an important source of the party's legitimacy, especially after the declining significance of communism after Deng's reform. Henceforth, Chinese nationalism is driven from two directions: state nationalism from the top down that is pragmatic, synonymises state interests with that of the nation, emphasises economic growth, political stability and national unity; and popular nationalism from the bottom up, which is particularly mistrustful of everything foreign while keeping a critical watch on the competency of the state in guarding the national interest (Zhao 2013). Indeed, a multi-country survey conducted in 2008 showed that China has 'one of the highest levels of nationalism in the world' (Tang and Darr 2012).

Within this backdrop of rising tides of nationalistic sentiment in China, some have postulated that the middle class will be aggressively nationalistic, as they are the main consumers of popular and state nationalist ideas, to the extent that even if they push for democratisation, the end result will still be xenophobic and anti-America (Friedman and McCormick 2015). Meanwhile, there is also the empirical challenge that the middle classes in Beijing are actually more liberal than their counterparts, especially in their attitude towards foreign policies, such as reduction of tariffs and military expenditure (Johnston 2004). In terms of how the Chinese middle class see themselves with regard to their national identity, and how they view their neighbours and other superpower nations that are particularly wary of China' rise, however, the picture remains unclear. In this chapter, I posit these questions to the middle class respondents of Ningbo, and try to shed better light on how the Chinese middle class see themselves in the context of what is Chinese, and what is foreign.

Endogenous conceptions of being 'Chinese'

To explore how the middle class view and understand themselves in the context of being Chinese, they are assessed through their opinions on traditional culture, the idea of Chinese exceptionalism, and any elements of cultural superiority. Some of the survey questions are adapted from the Pew Global Attitudes Survey, to allow a brief comparison with national trends, where possible. The results from Table 5.1 reveal a mixed image. First, there is a strong association with what is seen as traditional Chinese values and a noticeable tendency to feel that Chinese culture is being threatened by consumerism, almost exactly on a par with the Pew national sample of 57 per cent (Pew 2012), which suggests a strong commitment to the preservation of tradition. Second, the roughly 50–50 split on the idea of Chinese exceptionalism and cultural superiority suggests that there is a lack of consensus on the topic, although it should be noted that the amount of support for Chinese cultural superiority is lower than that of the Pew national sample, which indicates that 77 per cent of the total respondents believed Chinese culture to be superior than others (Pew 2011). A third and perhaps most outstandingly, despite the tentative display of nationalistic sentiments above, only less than a third would advocate a way of life free from foreign influence, which is significantly less than the Pew sample of 2012, which rendered 71 per cent of the respondents who believed the same (Pew 2012).

Since the Pew Global survey was also not a nationally representative sample, only a tentative comparison can be drawn between that and the sample from this study, which suggests that the middle class are less prone to ethnocentric sentiments, and most notably, are significantly less likely to reject foreign influence. This finding is largely consistent with existing middle class literature that asserts the 'global' nature of the rising middle class in developing countries, arguing that their new found affluence, higher education and contact with the West have made them increasingly receptive to the effects of globalisation (Lange and Meier 2009; Kharas and Gertz 2010). Yet, the added questions in this survey, which address the

Table 5.1 Attitude towards Chinese nationalism

Statement	% of valid supportive responses
Favourable to tradition	
I still subscribe to traditional Chinese values such as Confucian and Taoist ideas.	82.2
Consumerism and commercialism pose a threat to Chinese culture.	56.4
Chinese exceptionalism	
China has a unique set of values; foreign values are unsuited for China.	54.3
We should protect our ways of life from foreign influence.	26.4
Cultural superiority	
Although imperfect, Chinese culture is still superior to other cultures of the world.	49.4

issue of middle class attitude towards the so-called 'Chinese values', indicates that the Chinese middle class have retained strong national and cultural-specific values and simultaneously are receptive to global influences. Indeed, interviews revealed that the meaning of Chinese values is both elusive as it is definitive: as with the Chinese national identity, its formation is an interactive process, brought out of the contrast between the 'self' and the 'other', the 'past' and the 'now'.

Chinese values versus universal values

Similar to how many respondents formed their own subjective class identity according to, and against, what they imagined to be the 'ideal middle class', their idea of what Chinese values are is often shaped by the imagined 'universal' Western values. Whereas they often struggled to come up with concise and clear descriptions of what the former contains, the respondents could often make a list of what they believed to be principal elements of 'universal values' with little hesitation: individualism, democracy and freedom being prime contenders. The inability to reach a consensus about the value system inherent to their own cultural environment does not deter from their belief that such value systems exist; in fact, it is precisely because the value system exists, and is perceived to be evolving fast in the globalised environment, that its current, updated definition is rendered difficult. Thus, 'Chinese values' are less tangible than they are contextualised: they are both compared longitudinally with its past, and in parallel with the West. The Confucian notions of filial piety and respect for elders, two of the most frequently referenced values inherent to the Chinese, for example, were contrasted against the imagined Western values of 'mutual independence' among generations, where parents would encourage children to be independent at the earliest opportunity, and in turn do not expect their children to take care of them in old age. The latter, viewed as a lack of moral and sentimental obligation, was frowned upon by many. The contrast was often highlighted to bring out the 'human touch' of Chinese values, with its focus on social ties and human relationships, as opposed to individual interest and contractual relationships.

The socially inclined, moderate nature of Chinese values has further implications. In older respondents' eyes in particular, Chinese values are the antithesis of violent expansionism, which they believe underlines 'foreign', most notably America's, values. America's 'propensity to start regional wars' and 'impose their values upon others' was often used as a counter example to China's value of 'middlebrow', as they believed China has lack of similar ambitions. America's involvement in Afghanistan and Iraq was heavily criticised, as the respondents argued that 'the people there are no better off' and that 'America should keep their domestic affairs in order first'. By contrast, they described that China would 'prosper without expanding borders', arguing that expansionism is not natural to Chinese culture. Instead, they believed the attention of a strong nation on the rise should be focused inward, on people's livelihoods, instead of outward into other nation's affairs. The emphasis on domestic socioeconomic prosperity resonates with the idea of 'people-based governance', which traditionally saw the state's legitimacy being derived from its ability to meet the people's needs – i.e. the ability to live and work in peace. One frequently raised example was America's disaster relief effort for Hurricane Katrina, which was seen as 'woefully inadequate' compared to China's 'efficient' disaster relief effort in the Wenchuan earthquake of 2008. Thus, the respondents came to associate Western values with overconfidence and arrogance, as opposed to humility and moderation as taught by Chinese traditional values. In the context of American diplomacy, these respondents definitely view China as 'pandas', not 'dragons', and are generally convinced of its peaceful rise.

While such differences between Chinese and Western values are the product of the respondent's imagination, it is not simply a function of ignorant stereotyping. In fact, most answers given were remarkably well thought-out, if somewhat unsystematic: the contrast between the atheist aspect of Confucianism and the monotheism of Abrahamic religions, for example, is particularly shrewd. Kosei argued that whereas the West had Abrahamic religion, China had Confucianism and Taoism, which served in the capacity of faith, but without the implications of traditional organised religion. This point was particularly important, she argued, because in monotheism, God was seen as a supreme, unsurpassable deity, and no humans could be its equivalent, whereas Confucianism encouraged the Chinese to adhere to the 'heavenly way', and try to be the heavenly way, or even surpass it through personal effort. Although not all of the respondents were able to raise their argument to such an abstract level, frequent references were made to the Confucian aspiration of benevolence, and the gentleman, the Taoist idea of harmony, and to a lesser extent the Buddhist goal of enlightenment, which arguably helps to create a different, more coherent and less antagonistic world view than that offered by Abrahamic religions, which are largely dualistic and result in an 'either/or' mode of thinking (Nadeau 2013).

Consequently, it is of little surprise that the respondents came to associate Western, universal values with implicit standards: one is either in accordance of these values (free, democratic and equal) or one is not. Many had no problem admitting that they subscribe to the principles of so-called universal values; the only setback was that they did not believe these values were in fact universal, much less 'universal' by American standards. It is generally believed that America is propagating so-called 'universal values' based on their own belief systems, which are widely frowned upon, as the respondents preferred to think that there is no one-size-fits-all value system suitable for the world, Chinese values included. Instead, they argued that many aspects of Chinese and Western values were not, and should not be, mutually exclusive to one another, that a balance and compromise should be preferred over the dominance of one set of values over the other. It is frequently suggested that Western values of democracy and individualism are perhaps better on the macro-, exogenic level, but Confucian and Taoist values were better on a micro-, endogenic level: Abbey used the phrase 'democracy to rule the country, middlebrow as a way of life', while William said that 'one should live according to the Chinese way, and do things according to the Western way'. These ideas stem from their criticism of both value systems: that Chinese values place too much emphasis on the society of the collective, while Western values over-emphasise the individual. Hence, they may be said to be pragmatic nationalists, as they believe Western values of individualism and Chinese values of society with a 'human touch' are seen to complement each other well, as a combination of both would equalise the role of the individual and society, while retaining some features of community among individuals within that society. Of course, the very idea of balance-seeking and harmony is closer to the Chinese tradition in its root than the Western tradition, as one of the most crucial aspects of Chinese culture allowing its continued survival is its ability to adapt by finding a workable balance in the face of foreign influx. Considered from this angle, the very act of finding a compromise could in fact be a reflection of the Confucian 'middlebrow'.

The inability to pinpoint the cultural and value aspects of being Chinese is partly due to its complexity and vastness, but also due to its evolvement and interaction with the outside world. The respondents are keenly aware of the effect of foreign influence upon China, in terms of both its convenience and horizon-broadening experience and its potential 'pitfalls'. Thus, while foreign influence was not entirely unwelcome, many respondents specified that only the 'good aspects' of foreign culture should be imported, rather than introducing everything at once. Among the 'pitfalls', individualistic heroism and hedonism were outlined as undesirable and corrupting, while the rule of law and attention paid to human rights were seen as 'worthy of study'. Kun disliked the 'blatant Americanism' displayed through blockbuster films and mainstream media, which the respondents saw as 'just another form of propaganda'. Among the more moderate, Abbey and Lily felt that the permeation of cultures is a natural selection process, so any aspects of foreign influence allowed in would naturally be the 'essence' rather than 'drivel'. Wang argued that in the era of globalisation, the convergence of cultures is inevitable and cannot be held back; thus, it is incumbent on the individual to discern between the good and the undesirable. The common theme among all, nevertheless, was the need for caution and selection, not blanket acceptance, again in the pragmatic vein. Lu commented:

> [To learn from the West] you need an integrating process, can't just dump their ideas everywhere. The West came a long way as well, they had their fair share of invasions, violence, instability and bloodshed, so we will get there too.

Romanticising the past

Tradition is by definition juxtaposed against the modern; hence, 'traditional Chinese values' of the present day should be compared against its historical roots and an imagined, more pristine form. Part of the reason given for their inability to explain what Chinese values really are is that these traditions and values have been continuously eroded and challenged throughout history, especially in the twentieth century. Indeed, when asked if Chinese tradition is being preserved in present day China, the outlook reflects the uncertainty that the respondents feel about the definition of Chinese values as a whole. While very few were certain that Chinese traditional culture had been lost (2.8 per cent), a fair number of the respondents veer towards the pessimistic side, either believing that it is disappearing (39.8 per cent), and a similar number believe that despite the various political and educational movements to get rid of the so-called drivel in traditional culture, it has been preserved along with the essence (35.9 per cent). Only 17.1 per cent of the surveyed respondents believe that has for the most part preserved the essence of traditional culture, and fewer than 5 per cent believe that the culture is mostly preserved in its entirety (4.4 per cent).

Among the components of traditional culture that were deemed lost, the 'five constant virtues' of benevolence, righteousness, propriety, wisdom and fidelity were cited the most. The preoccupation with these virtues accords with the respondents' general concern over moral decay in society, as these virtues are supposed to guide a person's moral behaviour. This emphasis is in contrast with the three cardinal guides, which dictated the subordinate relationships between the king and the subject, the father and the son, and the husband and the wife, that the respondents believed should be rightfully abandoned except the idea of filial piety, as the rest was seen as no longer fitting with modern society. Family values, however, were considered to be the strongest surviving traditions of China, especially in comparison with the West. Some attributed its survival to the continued use of proverbs such as 'an old person is a treasure in a household', carried down through generations in the same family units it advocated, while others believed that the idea of filial piety is conducive to social stability; therefore, filial piety was never challenged by the state. Nevertheless, its survival was seen as in the minority, as personal virtues, the 'inner morality' that the five constant virtues sought to represent, were widely considered endangered, and to some, were deemed to be irrevocably lost.

Whereas academics have attributed the changing landscapes of morality in China to the transition between a *geimenschaft* community to a *gesellschaft* society (Kleinman *et al.* 2011), the rise of individualisation and such structural factors (Halskov, Hansen and Svarverud 2010), these middle class respondents advocated the view that modern society lacked a 'moral watchdog' similar to the intelligentsia of the old. Jane argued that due to the rise of social media and the mass influx of sensational stories, society is becoming apathetic to morally condemnable behaviours, and is now considering the abnormal to be the norm. The emphasis was that it is now the norm for people to take pride in their opportunistic gains and casual flaunts, rather than 'being ashamed as they should'. It is lamented that the cost of upholding virtues was increasingly high in a morally apprehensive society: when people run a risk of being penalised for good deeds, they will either avoid doing so and 'keep their heads low', or seek to minimise their chance of penalisation by becoming allied with the punisher. Often, the respondents expressed resignation as they believed that because people cannot change society, when society changes, they have no choice but change along with it. In a similar vein, Jane drew a keen comparison between the *literati* (scholar-bureaucrats) of the old, and the successful of the modern day.

> In the Song dynasty, the *literati* all had a special air around them – a certain kind of principle and morality. They can keep true to themselves, and society respected the famous *literati*. Back then, they were not famous because of their money, but their knowledge, ability and talent; their personal traits. Today's society judges people by whether someone's got money and power. But to be a *literatus*, someone has to have money, power, as well as knowledge and talent. Prime Ministers back in the Song dynasty had real talent. While the successful people nowadays have their own talent, they lack a certain kind of respect for knowledge and freedom, the insistence of 'self', the upholding of their personal beliefs.

To others, the breaking of tradition was the result of a more recent, conscious political effort. From the early 20th century attempt to Westernise in Republican China to the breaking of the 'Old Four' in the Cultural Revolution, several respondents noted that these various political movements had created a visible 'cultural chasm'. The Cultural Revolution, for example, was seen to have 'kneecapped the very classes, the landlords and the councillors that had access to traditional knowledge, and would otherwise uphold traditional virtues'. As virtue and tradition were passed down through generations and family, in an era when access to education was still limited to the rich, the removal of the landed gentry inevitably results in the 'cultural break' seen in China today. Furthermore, some remembered how Mao's political movements made society 'black and white', or rather 'black and red', so that everyone was labelled clearly and there were no grey areas. Several believed such extreme categories were the polar opposite of Confucian teachings, the need to be middlebrow, which led

84 *Nationalism among the middle class*

not only to confusion but intolerance in Chinese society. Such confusion is perhaps deserved, as Wang commented:

> In the old times, we had the doctrine of Confucius and Mencius. Doesn't matter if you think it's a form of spiritual shackles or a moral compass, it has kept us in line. But in the most recent century, it has been overturned and critiqued … tradition has been broken and nothing new has yet replaced it. What's the core value for socialism? I don't know. I don't think there is one. Back in Confucius' time, the five constant virtues were the core values, and everyone operated according to that, especially regarding interpersonal relationships. This has been overturned. What's new? Nothing. Maybe democracy, science, freedom, or Sun Yatsen's Three Principles of the People, but we don't accept that, do we? So, what do we accept? Love for the state and the Party?
>
> —*Wang*

Again, as previously mentioned regarding welfare and the role of the state, this general moral decay in society is seen as a side effect of China's economic reforms. The rise of monetarism and utilitarianism as the new benchmark for success, as opposed to the Confucian virtues, was particularly frowned upon. Consumerism was seen as an unavoidable byproduct of reform, and a threat to the virtuous values such as austerity and frugality, especially in the coastal cities. Some believed that the lull of excessive consumption was so tempting that even if values of frugality were still preserved in inland areas, it was more likely because they were unable to afford to waste, rather than consciously choosing not to be wasteful. Min commented that 'traditional values are not lost, per se, but people are unwilling to adhere to it'. A change in habit due to the shift towards a consumerist society was identified as the main reason behind this unwillingness, along with a lack of education and family background. The advent of the Internet and the rapid dissemination of information were also seen as a double-edged sword: on the one hand, it broadened people's horizons; on the other hand, the rapid influx of imported values made it difficult for people to 'differentiate between the good and the bad'.

In a similar vein, Wang proposed that the post-reform 'moral decay' had its roots in Deng's famous cat theory. He believed that such ideas encouraged people to focus on the end result, using whatever means necessary to achieve said results. People forgo 'proper proceedings and justice' in face of profit, and profit became the highest order of morality. China's under-developed legal system is unable to deal with such moral decay, so that 'people's good sides are being suppressed, and their evil side allowed to emerge – even encouraged'. Indeed, the peril of consumerism was such that 'values changed too quickly', that 'nothing was constant except money'. Kun's wistful comment is illustrative of this line of reasoning:

> When you have the reforms, everyone starts to align their views and faith towards money. Society changes too fast, even for someone relatively young as me (33 years old), I can't keep up, I don't know what to follow. Money

is the only constant, success is measured by nothing but money. That's why morals are lacking nowadays, because you can't go slow any more. Sometimes you are just pressured to follow whatever is out there.

As a result, some respondents based their interpretation of Chinese values on a practical, pessimistic observation of modern society, arguing that the value of Chinese society is now money-oriented, utilitarian and heavily reliant on *guanxi*. Abbey noted that modern Chinese values are fundamentally about money because 'nowadays most people would judge others' success by their accumulated wealth', to the extent that the importance of money surpasses education, which once directed and shaped one's values. After all, the term 'value' (*jiazhi guan*, 价值观) denotes *one's worth* at the very fundamental of its meaning. It is observed that utilitarianism has also tainted people's beliefs, because 'if people claimed to believe, they believed it for some kind of reward – whether it's for karma or for their spiritual protection.' Aline further argued that money and *guanxi* were inseparable as the core values Chinese people lived by in today's society, since they were both the indicators and influencers of one's success. For those who believed and criticised the present as such, they conveyed that monetarism and nepotism have since replaced traditional Chinese virtues as the new moral guidelines for society.

Despite their disappointment in the current state of cultural preservation, many respondents also noted that traditional Chinese culture is experiencing a revival. One respondent believed the complete Westernisation and abandonment of Chinese tradition during the Republican era were largely due to 'the weakness in the nation', and as China become stronger, the revival of tradition was to be expected. Indeed, many registered a renewed interest in Sinology classes and ancestral worship, and commented widely on the study of classics in classrooms in primary and secondary education. However, the respondents were dubious about how much of these revivals were in 'form' and how much in 'spirit'. Sarcastic remarks were made about how it was becoming a fashion to reacquaint oneself with so-called Sinology at the management level, which they believed was a superficial attempt to appear cultured, rather than a genuine interest in traditional Chinese culture and values. The act of casual worship also garnered certain confusion: Min and Jessie observed that many people around them, sometimes themselves included, would perform acts of worship in Buddhist, Taoist and ancestral temples alike, regardless of its origin. To them, the act was learned and carried out, but whether the underlying values were still the same was debatable. The dilemma was that they felt these behaviours were traditionally considered as a reflection of Chinese values, but that might no longer be the case. Nevertheless, nearly all of the interviewed respondents admitted that they 'accepted traditions on a subconscious level', regardless of whether they followed through with the ritualistic aspect or not.

For these middle class respondents, they remembered China's past like China's classical historians: with a tendency to romanticise. They looked to ancient China (a vague and undefined concept) as the 'superior times', and considered Chinese culture to be *once* superior to others, although the public discourse on hundred

86 *Nationalism among the middle class*

years of humiliation has led them to believe that this superiority has ceased to be the case. The most frequently cited historical 'achievements' include the four great discoveries of paper, gunpowder, the compass and live printing; Chinese classical writings and traditional medicine; and Chinese culinary culture. At some point in the transition towards modernity, groundbreaking discoveries ceased to be made; intangible cultural heritages began to decline; and only Chinese culinary culture remained flourishing across the world, although most respondents did not consider it to be a form of soft power worth comparing. Nostalgia aside, there is also a considerable amount of confusion as to how, why and to what extent that superiority had been eroded. Like their opinion on Chinese values as a whole, the respondents' views of the past could at best be described as a vague and imprecise 'feeling', which nevertheless is used to underpin their national identity.

Exogenous conception of the 'other'

In addition to exploring the respondents' national identity in terms of their sense of 'self', they were asked to rate their feelings towards several countries on a scale of 1 to 10, 1 being 'hostile', 5 being 'neutral' and 10 being 'friendly', in order to explore their attitude towards the 'other' (Figure 5.1). Three countries were included in the question set: Japan, America and India. Two more sensitive regions were added for the interviewees: North Korea and the Philippines (in relation to the South China Sea).

Japan

Of the three countries, the respondents presented most animosity towards Japan: 36 per cent chose the most hostile end of the scale (1). The hostile side of the scale received 59 per cent of votes, while only 7 per cent of the respondents felt a degree of friendliness towards the nation, and 32 per cent were neutral. A greater

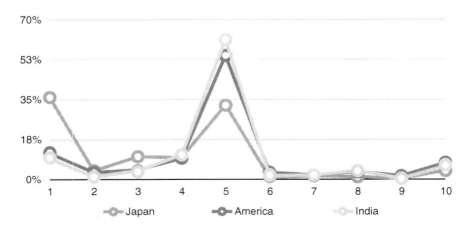

Figure 5.1 Attitude towards foreign countries

proportion of the self-ascribed salaried class respondents felt extreme animosity towards Japan compared to their middle class counterparts: 40 per cent on the scale of 1 compared to 29 per cent, respectively. Among those who felt a certain degree of hostility towards Japan, the respondents felt both wary of its political and military ambition, which was seen as 'aggressive' and 'unrepentant', and they expressed anger towards Japan's treatment of its war crimes in World War II. The same respondents who advocated for rationality and logic when approaching incidents such as PX in Zhenhai nevertheless turn passionate, as shown below:

> I read about a professor saying that there will inevitably be a war between China and Japan. I believe that Japan as a nation is fundamentally different to that of other nations in Southeast Asia. Why does Germany have no problem admitting their war crimes? Japan wouldn't admit anything. They've fought wars with every single neighbour they have, Korea, Russia, Mongolia, even America. They always grumble about the fact that two atomic bombs were dropped on them, but it's their fault! They invaded other people in the first place! If they cannot see that, they will forever be an agent of instability [in the region].
>
> —*Lu*

The emotional language used by these respondents suggests that they are very much subscribed to the public discourse of humiliation and victimisation. William and Wang both proposed that Japan had been a wolf and that China had been a sheep, which in their eyes summarised the reason and outcome of the Sino-Japanese War. By extension, they argued that no matter how strong China gets economically, if the 'sheep mentality' does not change, she will perpetually be vulnerable to threat from another wolf attack. Those who grew up with anti-Japanese propaganda were particularly in favour of this idea:

> I'm very unfriendly towards Japan. It's very deep rooted. All my childhood I had dreams where Japanese soldiers were chasing me. Watched too many films.
>
> —*Lily*

For many, their main grievance was Japan's refusal to apologise for its war crimes, and Japanese Prime Minister Shinzo Abe insistence on visiting the Yasukuni Shrine where many war criminals were being worshipped. The sense of annoyance and wrongdoing was further exacerbated by the dispute over Diaoyu Islands, which some saw as 'aggravating' and 'deliberate'. Aline, who works in an import/export company, professed that her friendliness towards Japan had dropped since the survey, because renewed dispute over Diaoyu Islands had reminded her of some negative experience in dealing with Japan in the past:

> When I did the survey, I gave them a four. Right now I think I'd only give them a one. Because of the Diaoyu conflict – regardless of history, which, by the way, totally stakes China's claim – I feel the Japanese are much more anti-Chinese than we are anti-Japanese. They've refused to turn up to Expos

and cancelled their trips to China. When we are doing business with the Japanese, I've heard that they say they'd give the Koreans a good price, but they wouldn't budge a dime for the Chinese. Because they know we know their goods are of superior quality, and they know we'd buy them even if the price is high. We wouldn't really boycott their goods, whereas the Koreans can and will. The way they treat us is despicable.

Nevertheless, these respondents were still able to make a clear distinction between Japanese culture, which some admired, and Japanese politics, which was met with universal contempt. Even those who showed the strongest dislike towards Japan (mainly because of its politics) admitted a reluctant admiration for the 'unity' and *suzhi* of their people, which makes Japan a formidable opponent in their eyes. The Japanese people were often referred to as 'courteous', 'law-abiding', and 'with great self-control' while Japanese culture was seen as 'orderly', 'united', 'civilised', albeit with a 'strong sense of militarism'. Wang, who had travelled to Japan on business, found the trust and self-regulation in society remarkable:

I often went drinking with my colleagues in Japan after work, and we would take a taxi home. The company would pay for the taxi fare, so when we got off, we would sign a piece of paper and submit it to the taxi driver, noting how much the trip cost, and the driver would be reimbursed from the company. Every Japanese colleague of mine just gave the driver the paper and asked him to complete it – I was very surprised. I asked them, what if the driver claimed more than what the journey actually cost? They were also surprised, and told me that it would never happen. It's a society based on trust.

When we went to Tokyo, we also took a taxi, and we asked the driver to wait for us at one of the scenic spots while we toured for a while. That's unimaginable in China – you'd worry about the taxi driver leaving you, and the taxi driver would worry about you leaving him. This society of trust takes a long time to develop – China is far from that yet.

Even Aline expressed reluctant admiration for Japan's national unity amid her overall hostile attitude:

Japan is rather disgusting. Their people are very united, though, as is their country. They say one Chinese man is a dragon, but ten Chinese men is a worm. We are not as united as they are. They also have a good preservation of tradition, their handcraft industry, their manufacturing and electronics, the quality is very good, tightly controlled. We don't have that either. But we have a historical grudge against them. People of my generation, and my parent's, definitely don't like the Japanese. I've been to Japan twice, and although the Japanese people I met were nice and courteous, you can tell from the way they look at you that they really despise you at heart. They don't treat us as equals.

Nationalism among the middle class 89

The perceived combination of aggressive tendencies and admirable self-discipline is what makes Japan a formidable opponent – it has both the ambition and the means to be threatening. Consequently, Japan should be watched for, but also learned from – a few respondents used the phrase 'subdue the enemy by learning from their strong points', which was popularised in the Self-Strengthening Movement in the Qing Dynasty, to describe their desired approach towards Sino-Japanese relations.

Despite these grievances, however, the majority of the surveyed respondents did not advocate a violent solution to the key issue in Sino-Japanese relations: the Diaoyu (Senkaku) Islands conflict. When asked to choose a statement closest to their attitude and behaviour towards the conflict, Table 5.2 shows that 65 per cent supported a diplomatic resolution of the matter, and only 20 per cent argued for armed resolution. Although there was widespread boycotting of Japanese goods and anti-Japanese demonstrations elsewhere in China, fewer than 20 per cent professed that they took part in this Ningbo sample. Again, there was a bigger proportion of salaried class respondents who preferred this option, which is consistent with the larger proportion of those respondents who were hostile towards Japan. Understandably, more of those working within the state sector and had CCP memberships held more moderate views on the issue and were more supportive of diplomatic resolution.

Among the interviewed respondents, even though some like Lu believed there will eventually be a war between Japan and China, no respondent actively advocated for war. Some felt a stalemate would be beneficial because the problem 'clearly could not be solved by their generation', citing Deng's famous speech that the Diaoyu dispute should be 'left to the later generations'. The elder respondents in particular felt that 'if the great politicians such as Zhou Enlai and Deng Xiaoping could not have solved the problem, the current generation could not either.' Furthermore, most respondents pointed out that to declare war would be mutually destructive for both nations. They were typically aware of America's

Table 5.2 Choose the closest statement that describes your attitude towards the Diaoyu Islands conflict (n=181)

Statement	Salaried class (%)	Middle class (%)	Overall (%)
I boycotted Japanese goods and cars, and participated in the anti-Japanese movement.	25.7	14.1	19.7
I believe the matter of Diaoyu Islands should be solved diplomatically and by the government.	62.1	66.7	64.5
This is a matter of concern for the state, not for me.	5.4	7.7	6.6
I believe the matter of Diaoyu Islands should be resolved by armed resolution.	24.3	16.7	20.4
Other	6.8	0	3.3

involvement in the region and its potential ability to 'muddy the waters', citing severe economic and political ramifications in the event of war. Wang argued for a status quo based on such grounds:

> The problem of Diaoyu Islands should be put on hold. We should maintain the status quo. War is the least favourable option. I don't think we will go to war: China's current economic development relies too heavily on foreign investment, trade and import – such as oil and energy. This is a pillar for our economy. If we go to war, foreign trade will take a severe hit, so we are not doing ourselves any favours. Going to war with Japan is practically going to war with America – they are allies. Is it necessary to go to war with America over Diaoyu Islands? The price is too steep. Some people say, 'I'd rather lose decades of development than see the island lost', but that's just angry words. If you actually did that, you are an idiot.

Although the respondents made passing remarks on China's increasing military prowess as an element of national pride, few mentioned it with the Diaoyu question in mind. Only one respondent, Kosei, felt certain that Japan is 'scared of China' and believed the outcome of war would be favourable in Chinese odds, but even then she did not see it as a reason to go to war. She, too, advocated for a stalemate on the grounds that 'all roads would lead to peace talks':

> [We should] wait and see ... if America becomes weak and abandons Japan, and China becomes stronger, then we can solve the problem through peace talks. If China weakens and Japan gets stronger, then we must negotiate with them anyway. War always comes with unpleasant side effects.

Although none of the respondents felt that China's renewed military strength is a reason for starting a war, several respondents emphasised that they were not afraid to meet Japan's provocations, should the need arises. Referring often to historical grudges between the two countries, phrases such as 'China is stronger now' and 'we can longer be bullied' were often used. Their pride in China's military development seems to be in national defence, rather than offence, and their language suggests that the history of the Sino-Japanese war still leaves an impact on their 'bullied' mentality.

> The state says we protest vehemently [to their provocations], so we protest. What else can we do? At the end of the day, war would never benefit the *laobaixing*. We don't want war. But if they push us too far, then we have to fight! We can't take prerogative because you need to make sure you can fight a winning war. But if they keep pushing, then we need to defend ourselves. Like Chairmao says, 'we will not attack unless attacked first'.
>
> —*Lily*

Many respondents referred to the idea of China's peaceful rise and the nation's disinclination for war, often as a counterexample to the aggressive ambitions of

Japan and America. Again, 'traditional Chinese values' were cited in support of their claim – some invoked Confucian notions of middlebrow, others used the example of the Great Wall and argued that it was always a 'defensive structure', illustrating China's pacifist history. Whether those beliefs are true is another matter: the fact remains that most respondents are adamant that China is 'different' from Japan and America. Although their language is nonviolent and the general dislike of armed conflict is palpable, their view towards Japan is still acutely adversarial and wary.

On a more practical side, several respondents felt that although diplomatic resolution is desired, China must show a stronger hand in the diplomatic exchange. A few respondents mentioned Russia, and how China should learn from its 'iron-fist' policy. Abbey criticised China's current policy as making the country a 'soft fruit for Japan to squeeze', while Russia's adamant attitude is more beneficial. Jane held a similar view:

> China's diplomatic efforts are too soft … Learn from Putin, I say! Russia's territory is vast, but they have not a single, extra inch. Japan retreats so fast when Russia contests any piece of land, even if Russia did invade it.

The respondents' knowledge of the Diaoyu issue varied from person to person. Some clearly have a good understanding of the overall causation-event chain, while others base their opinions on hearsay. Several were entirely uninterested in the Diaoyu issue: Kun believed the government simply uses the Diaoyu dispute as a tool to encourage national unity, while Min and Jessie had very little opinion on it, due to lack of interest. Nevertheless, they all expressed an aversion towards war, which they believed is shared among the Chinese and the Japanese. Jessie's comment illustrates their viewpoint best:

> I don't want war, of course, who wants war? The Japanese don't want war. I'll have to run to Tibet if we start a war. I don't care about who gets Diaoyu Islands, though. As long as they don't affect me.

All of the respondents agreed that boycotting Japanese goods was 'useless' and 'irrational', although some thought that the people had a right to boycott while others believed it should be discouraged. None of the interviewed respondents took part in the boycotts or the demonstrations, some for idealistic reasons (against the irrationality of boycott) and others for pragmatic reasons (impractical to give up Japanese car or Japanese electronics, which were 'a good value for the money'). All of the respondents condemned the violence that broke out during the anti-Japanese demonstrations, and denounced such actions as 'irrational nationalism (*feilixing aiguozhuyi,* 非理性爱国主义)'. Wang explained the phenomenon in the following manner:

> The anti-Japanese movement and the smashing of Japanese cars are just people expressing their frustration – the movement consisted of people

with differing outlooks and motivations. The demonstration itself should be allowed, that's normal – people should be allowed to express their opinions. But smashing people's cars is unnecessary; it's private property. China nowadays ... nationalism or ethnocentrism, whatever you call them, they are all rearing their heads. For every ten yuan of Japanese goods, three or four must belong to the Chinese. The Japanese companies do hire Chinese workers, don't they!

America

The respondents' attitude towards America can best be described as 'friendlier', but with sufficient rationality and neutrality to acknowledge both its successes and shortcomings. Indeed, many respondents' first reaction towards America was 'better than Japan', and went on to explain that there had been very few direct confrontations between China and America in recent memory; hence, 'there is no real hatred'. The neutrality and amicability towards America largely rely upon being untainted with politics, as expressed below:

> I feel slightly more friendly towards the Americans than the Japanese. Because with the Japanese we have a political bone to pick, don't we, but with the Americans, all they're doing is shouting about the China threat and things like that. They bombed us once [the embassy in Yugoslavia], but that's about it. I like American shows though! I see no reason to dislike them too much, or be overly friendly.
>
> —*Jessie*

For those who expressed admiration towards America, they were particularly receptive towards American soft power, and contrasted areas of 'modernity' against China's corresponding 'backwardness'. Resource sufficiency without an exploding population, clear air and environment, better regulated society leading to better food safety and consumer security, as well as the rule of law are the most commonly cited aspects of American success, as opposed to objective identifiers such as advancements in sciences, medical care or even education. Some argued that their admiration for America could be backed up by popular observation, as an increasing number of people are now flocking to the U.S. to work, study or immigrate. Both Aline and Kun asked the rhetorical question, 'If America isn't as good as people say it is, why do people keep going?' To them, the observable phenomenon of the brain drain speaks louder than any ideological propaganda or hearsay one might encounter about the U.S.

> I do feel America is the pinnacle of humanity, the way we should all follow. You should know that a lot of things we enjoy now come from America, from inventions to ideology. You can say America is a melting pot, but why do people flock to America? There must be a reason for it. I believe in the American

mode. The way they have regulations in society, I think it's a rational choice. At least, the slogans and motto they carry is closer to what I believe.

—*Kun*

Again, media influence played a significant role in people's opinion of America. Lily referred to a 'vague sense of likeability' from the 'information' she got on a daily basis, which was echoed by quite a few respondents. From popular culture such as films and television shows to news items, there are very few directly confrontational pieces about America, unlike Japan. Whereas shows featuring the Sino-Japanese war effort is still a strong genre in Chinese domestic television, American shows are largely imported and consumed in private: more often it is found on computers (downloaded), rather than on television; hence, its audience made the conscious choice to consume its contents and, thus, are more likely to be receptive of its ideas and culture.

Nevertheless, very few respondents viewed America with 'rose tinted glasses' and expressed their admiration without reservation. Many were able to explain neutrally that similar to all countries, America has its own problems, most noticeably gun crimes and hate crimes. The widely reported Hurricane Katrina at the time also shaped the respondents' opinion of the American government, which they believed was inadequate in its disaster management and relief. Contrast was drawn between Katrina and the Wenchuan earthquake, where the respondents viewed Chinese government's fast and efficient disaster response as a matter of national pride. America's debt to China was also mentioned frequently, but often with a joking air around it: several respondents quoted an Internet meme that whenever America criticised China, the standard response would be 'give our money back first!'

Indeed, many respondents acknowledged and respected America's advanced economic development and to an extent political development, but usually frowned upon America's exporting ideology and its aggressive, imposing stance as the 'leader of the free world'. Lu was most expressive among them, although his frequent use of the term 'imperialist' bears certain Red imprints of his age:

I'm not as enthralled with America as other people. I think they have their own drawbacks … They should not enforce their ideals upon others. Everyone lives differently, and it should be the same with different countries. Every country's system is formed due to thousands of years of history, geography, religion, everything. They can't say democracy is the best and force it on everyone. That's basically chauvinism and imperialism. For example, the First Gulf War, they had a reason to invade Iraq, because Iraq invaded Kuwait. But the Second Gulf War was completely unnecessary, it's like what happened with our own national hero Yue Fei, it's trumped up charges … Libya is worse, what's happening in Libya is essentially what happened when the Eight Power Allied Forces invaded us … Invading other countries, that's blatant imperialism. Why interfere with other countries' business? That's what the UN is for. That's how it works nowadays though, those with harder fists get whatever they want. But that doesn't mean it's right.

India

Whereas the attitudes towards developed countries such as Japan and America were overall befitting of the reactive, pragmatic, state nationalism propagated by the CCP, the discussion of developing countries quickly turned in a different direction. At first glance, the surveyed respondents showed a similar degree of neutrality and overall friendliness towards India. However, the respondents' rhetoric during interviews revealed a greater sense of prejudice and stereotype, even though they did not feel this warranted hostility per se. Their impression of India is that of disorder, poor hygiene, rigid caste systems and questionable safety for females, no doubt influenced by the media and the recent reporting of rape cases. These elements of stereotype are all 'backward', thus affirming the respondents' belief that India is a backward country. There was a clear note of contempt in some respondents' answers, best illustrated by Kosei's response:

> I'd give them a two. The impression they give is the terrible caste system they have, and the fact you can't eat cows there! So few public toilets, too, a country that's dirty and disorderly. Not to mention they often infringe upon China's borders, but their military prowess is weak. Their military equipment is more like an exhibition on world arms dealers (comes from all kinds of countries and sources). 'Screw your MacMahon line' is what I want to say to India.

Despite frequent border clashes with India in the past, there was a notable lack of political conviction in the respondents' answers. However, their answers were remarkably more xenophobic than theirs were for Japan and America, sometimes to alarming extents. One respondent made a comment about how India's fast growing population is 'contaminating the gene pool', 'diluting the elites', which is the reason for India's backwardness in the modern age. Another even remarked flippantly that countries like India should be 'eliminated', as it does not fit in with 'humanity's progression'. A few respondents who have had dealings with Indians professionally or have studied India from a more neutral vantage point also commented that they thought Indians were 'sly and cunning', and that they were worried about India's 'economic supremacy', due to its geographical closeness with China.

North Korea

It was curious to observe the respondents' attitude towards a country with very little objective data, and to see some of them draw parallels between North Korea and the red era of China under Mao. The majority of interviewed respondents reacted negatively towards North Korea, arguing that it was a country 'against modernity'. A few lamented that North Korea was supposedly China's only brother-in-arms left in the socialist camp, but even they agreed that 'the country was beyond help', so long as it carries on the current regime.

Nationalism among the middle class 95

The respondents frequently drew parallels between North Korea's autocratic regime and China's era of the cultural revolution, when centralised party ideology exerted absolute influence and control over people's lives. They argued that China had 'outgrown' such gross mistakes, whereas North Korea seemed intent on continuing and repeating the mistake. Many respondents mentioned that the 'textbook stories' they heard coming out of North Korea reminded them of the propaganda stories they were taught when growing up, but on a 'much more ridiculous scale'. The most cited stories were the ones where Kim Jong Un shot down an enemy plane by throwing a stone, and news items of miracles found across North Korea that were supposedly in support of the regime. These stories seriously undermined North Korea's reputation as a 'legitimate country' in their eyes, and made any political actions on North Korea's part all the more suspicious. The respondents typically argued that a country that openly ignores human rights and unrepentantly defies the 'international development trend' is akin to a madman and cannot be held accountable for his/her actions, which makes North Korea exceedingly dangerous. A popular Chinese saying is used to describe the phenomenon: those who are bare foot will not be afraid of those wearing shoes, as they have nothing to lose. Abbey commented:

> Not a single good thing is heard about this country … The other day I read that apparently they found over 20,000 trees in North Korea that had the words 'Long Live Kim Jong Un' engraved onto its trunk, and they are going to protect them as a heavenly sign or something. We did that trick in like, the Tang dynasty. The whole hero worship thing – not even worship, but deifying an individual – is very much against the development of modernity. It's terrifying to think their leader can throw a bomb at us at a whim – there's no check against his power, and that's unsettling.

Some respondents also accused North Korea of being 'ungrateful' in the face of continued Chinese assistance, and expressed contempt for such 'forgetfulness'. Aline mentioned China's involvement in defending North Korea against invaders in both the Ming dynasty and the Korean war, and denounced North Korea's ungratefulness. She believed that the North Koreans were 'deeply paranoid and adversarial' in nature, fuelled by their closed political regime. Unlike the case of Japan, only one respondent distinguished the North Korean people and the politics, while the rest thought the people would have been similarly indoctrinated beyond help in a closely monitored society. Lu's response was by far the most moderate, but even then he conceded that it was difficult to feel friendly towards such an irrational nation:

> North Korea is what the Ningbo people call a 'triangular stone'. It can't be set properly. It's a historical problem. I think if they don't reform politically and economically, they won't have a future. Without China's help, millions would starve. Their current dictatorship will never work. But the North Korean people are very good and honest, it's just their leaders are misguided. But if I was

to give them a number on the friendliness scale, well, we are supposed to be comrades in arms after all. I say a six. But I don't feel very amiable towards them, to be honest.

The Philippines and the South China Sea

In addition to the xenophobia displayed in the respondents' answers towards India and North Korea, the response towards the Philippines and territorial disputes over the South China Sea even turned belligerent. Contrary to the respondents' previous attitude towards Japan and the Diaoyu Islands conflict, very few mentioned the potential involvement of America in the South China Sea, and nearly all described the Philippines using negative, demeaning phrases that suggest a noticeable degree of prejudice. Whereas most respondents were able to show a degree of respect for Japanese culture and distinguished clearly between the people and its politics, no such reluctant respect or concession was made for the Philippines. Instead, the Philippines was belittled and often despised: words such as 'disgusting', 'repugnant' and 'annoying' were common in their answers. The respondents typically saw the Philippines as a nuance, a 'hoodlum' who keeps 'pestering China's borders', one that could, and some argue should, be 'taken care of' by using decisive military action. One respondent even compared the Philippines to a 'yakking mad dog', while Japan was seen as a 'silently scheming master', both of whom China has to look out for.

Whereas the respondents generally considered Japan to be a 'big nation' and were very aware of the consequences of going to war, very little similar caution was exercised when talking about the Philippines. While most respondents would still prefer to avoid war if possible, almost everyone expressed jingoistic sentiments such as 'if needed be, the Philippines should be taught a lesson'. Some respondents justified their view by arguing that the Diaoyu Islands conflict is a political one, whereas the South China Sea is a 'purely territorial one', and from which China cannot back down. Others felt certain that waging war against the Philippines would have favourable outcomes for China, whereas the same thing cannot be said for Japan. Jessie's flippant attitude towards the issue illustrates this point well:

> Diplomatically, everyone likes to bully the weak and defer to the strong. Small country like the Philippines? Pffft. If we ought to fight, then we fight. So what? The Diaoyu problem is between two super-nations. The South Sea problem is between a super-nation and a small nation. That's much easier to handle. Then again, we've always been lenient and merciful towards the small nations. The leaders will never go to war for the sake of their political careers.

Some again lamented that China's diplomatic approach is 'too soft' in these matters. Whereas the preference for a diplomatic solution in Japan's case is largely because of the terrible imagined costs of war, the case for the Philippines is completely flipped on its head, suggesting a certain level of rather alarming supremacist thinking on the respondents' part. Strongly opinionated though comparatively much more under-informed, the respondents' answers were often more heated than their answers on the Japan question.

> The Philippines is asking for it. China's diplomatic tactics are too soft! The way we look at the Philippines is probably the same as the way Japan looks at us. It's different from the Diaoyu problem – Japan is very militarily strong, and they did overtake the island. We took Huangyan island, really, but once we did, there's no giving back, that's how territorial disputes work. Everyone has his arguments. My husband thinks it should be resolved by war, but I don't know too much about it. I think a strong military advance aimed for shock, to put them in their place once and for all, is probably a good idea.
>
> —*Jane*

A few male respondents joked that if China had the military capacity, they would like to see all disputed territories return to China via strong handed means if necessary. One respondent admonished that 'it's all shop talk until [the Chinese] are capable of building an aircraft carrier', which is what he considered to be a necessary requirement for successful military engagement in the region. Nevertheless, he and several other respondents argued that China's supremacy in the region needed to be asserted 'at some point', for nothing else than the 'protection of first line coastal cities', which are the most economically developed in the country. Again, some of the respondents' attitudes are remarkably – also alarmingly – flippant in this regard, compared to their somber and more calculative attitude towards Japan.

> The South China Sea ... is directly relevant to our future use of resources and survival. We can't back off from that. Just do what we gotta do. If we have to go to war, fine, I'll contribute towards that, I'll pay into the war effort. Probably can't pick up a gun myself, but I'll do what I can. In fact, I feel like we should've gone to war ages ago. Small countries like the Philippines, Vietnam ... should've taken them a long time ago. We should learn from the Americans in this respect – if it's profitable, we go to war [laughs]. If we had the capability, why not fight Russia to get our lost territories back. Alas, it's not practical.
>
> —*Kun*

The *Chinese* middle class

Like their class identities, the national identity of these middle class respondents is also formed through contextualisation of the 'self' and the negotiation with the imagined 'other'. On the one hand, they are clearly receptive to foreign ideas by virtue of their education and foreign exposure, and most view the culture and soft power of developed countries in a positive light. On the other hand, they insist that they have retained a 'core' set of national identity and values, which are distinctive from the so-called 'universal values', which they see as a critical feature of the West. As such, they are more aware of what Chinese values are *not* rather than what they are, and often jump from one definition to another, confusing Confucian, Taoist and Buddhist teachings and grouping them indiscriminately under the umbrella term of 'tradition'. Furthermore, their romanticisation of the past means that they also believe so-called traditional Chinese values have been eroded, transformed and diluted in the last century, which leads to further hesitation and uncertainty in identifying what these values consist of. Thus, they are neither nativists who reject foreign influence wholesale, nor anti-traditionalists who prefer the boundless adoption of foreign ideals and socioeconomic models. They are, like the elites whose interests closely reflect theirs, pragmatists: for instance, foreign influence and traditional values should both be accepted, but only the 'good aspects'; freedom and democracy are not mutually exclusive of the current Chinese regime, but specificities, applicability and timing should be considered.

Nevertheless, while these middle class respondents want to maintain the 'middle road' by accepting ideals from both Chinese origins and the foreign, the actual realisation of this 'mix and match' often proves difficult. They were quick to criticise certain behaviours in society that appears to be adhering to 'traditional values' or 'Western values', but were in fact the act of pseudo-believers, either out of misguidance or as a tool of manipulation. They worried about the ethical and moral ambiguities in modern Chinese society, of which loss of traditional values plays a key part. Much like post-revolutionary Europe, when the *ancien regime* is torn down, confusion and struggle inevitably follows as to 'what next' – the state, which was incremental in dismantling the 'four old traditions' in the revolutionary era, was seen as ambiguous in its attitude towards values and tradition during the time these respondents were questioned. In an era of rapid knowledge dissemination, both the foreign and the traditional are battling their ground, it is only natural for the respondents to feel disoriented in face of a large influx of information, which they often feel ill-equipped to parse. Whether the new China Dream discourse and the return of focus on traditional values propagated by Xi's administration will sway their opinion one way or the other remains to be seen.

Again, the respondents' attitudes towards developed countries such as Japan and America generally satisfy what scholars have identified as key features of state nationalism in China: pragmatic, non-confrontational, largely reactive and utilises a combined narrative of 'national humiliation, lingering sense of insecurity and rising pride to achieve the common goal of a strong China' (Zhao 2004a). They were adversary to the idea of war, emphasised the distinction between culture and politics, while maintaining that any provocation will be met with firm defensive action. However, their attitudes towards developing countries such as India, North Korea and the Philippines are far more xenophobic, prejudiced and even belligerent. Here, their views bear more resemblance to popular nationalism from the bottom up: not only are they mistrustful of their developing neighbours,

Nationalism among the middle class 99

they often remark on how the state is being too soft in its diplomacy. Although the respondents often emphasised the terrible costs of war and the humanistic nature of their avoidance of military conflict, similar caution and altruism are suspiciously absent in their attitude towards the Philippines. They did not see the Philippines and other small nations of South East Asia as a legitimate threat or even a respectable foe, nor do their nationalistic pride allow such small nations to keep 'pestering' China. The language used in those answers immediately became patronising and arrogant, with an alarming flippancy that suggested they thought the costs and outcome of war warranted not the same level of consideration as it does with Japan and other super nations.

On the other hand, it should be noted that the respondents were extremely aware, and several even worried, about the real possibility of going to war with Japan, whereas no similar concerns were exhibited in the case of the Philippines. It is possible that the respondents felt safer to joke and flex their virtual nationalistic muscles over the Philippines than Japan, which is clearly a subject that they have not given as much thought as they did with the Diaoyu Islands question. Nevertheless, when these sets of attitudes are considered as a whole, it begs the question of how impartial and well informed their opinions on international affairs are – especially whether the adversity to war, in the case of Japan, is borne out of humanitarian concerns or out of practical considerations of probable defeat.

What does this mean, then, for China and its international relations? While one might think that the study of popular opinion is a futile attempt in China because it is not a democratic state, it would be naive to think that the Chinese state is entirely impervious to the opinions of its people. As numerous scholarly works on the subject have pointed out, the rallying point of nationalism is instrumental in securing state legitimacy in China. It is unlikely that the state would alienate its people and risk losing one of the key tools in promoting national unity by going against popular opinion in this regard. Just as it is unimaginable now that China would return to its revolutionary red era, it is equally unfathomable that the Chinese state would re-endorse a rhetoric of dichotomy where America, Japan or any of the major world powers are seen as the 'enemy' of the Chinese people. In other words, it is now unimaginable for China to 'relapse' into a state similar to North Korea.

Nevertheless, the question of Chinese nationalism should be understood both in terms of how the they view themselves, and how they view others. After all, national identity is still an identity; identities are fundamentally representations of 'self', aimed at 'others'. This point is especially relevant for the middle class, whose class identity also partially rests upon its broad contact with the outside world, whether in terms of consumption patterns, or their values. Thus, middle class nationalism in China should be viewed in context with both its class identity *and* national identity. They are receptive to foreign ideas and are well balanced in some of their world views consistent with the characteristics of their class; on the other hand, they remain deeply influenced by traditional Chinese values and adhere to a coherent Chinese national identity that divides clearly between 'us' and 'them'. How the Chinese middle class hope to solve the resulting contradiction is akin to how China has absorbed numerous sources of foreign influence over the years: by careful assimilation. Instead of 'leaning to one side', they are skilled in finding the middle road where they are able to assert their national identity, while being absorptive of foreign influence that is deemed helpful and good. The result is that the Chinese middle class are at once nationalistic and international; they are fully prepared to engage the world as they simultaneously remain identifiably Chinese on their own.

6 Viewing those below
The marginalised social groups

The previous chapters have dealt with how the middle class respondents mediated their identities and their roles, and their political aspirations in the context of China's changing economic and sociopolitical environment. This chapter considers their approach to some of the most socially divisive topics, such as the question of gender, and attitude towards homosexuality and migrant workers. These questions are important because they can prove most revealing. While these middle class respondents readily admitted the need and advantage for progressive values such as liberty, freedom, tolerance and social justice, they do not necessarily act according to these values, and they rationalise their non-action n the context of self-interest and pragmatic concerns at large. This chapters throws further and sharper light on such contradictions and paradoxes in the respondents' thinking, and illustrate how these middle class respondents try to negotiate a space between the self and the imagined 'collective'.

Gender

Gender is often a neglected theme in the discussion on globalisation and the rise of the middle class in East Asia. Yet, gender is inseparable from the integral processes that underline the making of the affluent middle class: changing consumption patterns, the clash of 'Western values' versus the 'traditional' values, and the reworking of the public and private spheres due to increased employment opportunities (and necessities) for women. The question of gender is particularly interesting in China because the country has had a period of history where women were desexualised, followed by the dramatic change of ideological environment that revolutionised the way women both viewed themselves and were viewed by society. Any effect that consumerism and globalisation might have on women in developing countries is no doubt exemplified in China.

The phenomenon of 'leftover women' is a recent one. Defined as 'women who remain unmarried over the age of 27' by China's All Women Federation (founded by the Chinese Communist Party (CCP) as a state feminist agency), the phrase was officially recognised by the Chinese Ministry of Education's lexicon in 2007, and has been the constant focus of media attention in recent years. At first glance, the increasing number of single, unmarried, often professional women in affluent Chinese cities seems to mirror a pattern that has been observed in similarly affluent Western cultures: the 'liberated' and 'independent' women, who choose to focus on their individual selves and their work, rather than the traditional family role (Beck 2002). The reality, however, is far more complicated. The term 'leftover women' alone sheds light into the patriarchal values and expectations that still remain in Chinese society today: it implies that women, when coming of age, becomes a commodity on the marriage market, and any woman over a certain age who remains unmarried is a 'leftover' item that failed to sell. Thus, the topic of 'leftover women' is highly controversial and gives insight to gender stereotypes, inequality and marriage stereotypes in Chinese society.

The overall trend presented in Table 6.1 is illuminative. Although the respondents' top choice in the four statements was that 'leftover women' is a derogatory term, nearly half of them also indicated that the key reason behind the phenomenon was the struggle over the work-family balance. This finding suggests two things: first, the respondents are largely aware of the 'double burden' that modern women face, with professional and household responsibilities. Second, the inability to deal with the double burden is considered as the reason for women being 'leftover' – this situation could imply that the respondents view these women as lacking in their ability to strive a healthy work-family balance, or they believe a choice or sacrifice has to be made. The considerable amount of support for this statement regardless of gender suggests an intense re-negotiation of the private and the public spheres, in the context of the 'traditional' (housewife) and the 'modern' (professional). Indeed, attitudes that border on the extreme such as 'some men are not worth marrying' and 'leftover women should be pitied' also gained around 10 per cent of support, illustrating the highly controversial and adversarial nature of the topic.

Table 6.1 Choose the closest statement that describes your attitude towards 'leftover women' (n=258)

Statement	Male (%)	Female (%)	Overall (%)
Women are often 'leftover' because they are too picky and have unrealisable standards.	30	18	22
Any woman who cannot find a suitor should be pitied.	9	7	8
'Leftover women' is a derogatory term; women should be allowed to make their own choices in marriage.	55	66	62
There are 'leftover women' because some men are simply not worthy to enter into marriage with.	7	14	12
It's too difficult for women to maintain a family life and a career in today's society; so, some of them are 'leftover'.	42	44	43

In accordance with the survey data, the interviewed respondents typically divided 'leftover women' into two groups: on the one hand, those who are too 'picky' and 'unrealistic' in their expectations of marriage partners, and on the other hand, those who are 'modern' and refuse to marry on principle. The impression was that most 'leftover' women fall into the first category, while those who insist on being single are in the minority, and stand out as being 'different'. The default assumption that women ought to marry, and should want to marry is commonplace: one respondent quoted a 'popular saying' that 'an unmarried woman is not whole'. Although the respondents typically hastened to add that they will not discriminate those who choose to remain unmarried, most of them also admitted that they would not have considered this option themselves, or would grant the freedom for their children to pursue a single life. Abbey commented:

> The idea of 'leftover' women implies that they weren't 'picked up' by the men, hence leftover. That's one type. Another type is actively choosing not to be picked, and that's different. If some women choose not to marry, well, that could be a modern feminist awakening. I personally don't understand it, but I won't discriminate against them ... I will be very worried if my daughter chooses to be single all her life, though. I'll probably try to set her up on dates ... but if it doesn't work, then what can you do?

More intriguing is the respondents' opinion on the first type of 'leftover women', who are seen as 'too picky' and 'unrealistic'. This is a very common belief, one that is even supported by the Chinese Ministry of Education in 2007. Although it appears they are placing the blame on women, the rhetoric actually presents a negative stereotype on men: many respondents, regardless of gender, argued that men in general are only concerned with beauty when choosing marriage partners, preferred their partner to be mild and obedient, and rejected women who are strong and independent. One respondent claimed:

> Men don't want to rely on a strong woman, when they see one, they'll think, 'well, I'm not good enough to marry you, and I don't want to bring you home to worship and hail you like some cadre leader either'. Sometimes women being too strong scares the men off.
>
> —*Junhui*

There seemed to be a consensus for women to 'marry up', and for men to 'marry down', which creates a mismatch between the two genders. A popular Internet saying was quoted often during interviews:

> Tier A men marry tier B women, tier B men marry tier C women, tier C men marry tier D women, and tier D men can't find wives. Tier A women certainly don't want to marry tier D men, so these they are the only two tiers 'leftover' in society. That's why there are so many professional, good-looking 'leftover women'!
>
> —*Xiaobo*

Several respondents further extrapolated that if a woman wants to marry too many tiers ahead – a C type woman wanting to marry A type man, for example – she would likely fail and be 'leftover' as people of her own league are married off. High expectations on the partner's income, physical appearance, level of education and place of work are all contributing factors to this 'unrealistic' checklist of the perfect partner, which was seen as the main obstacle in preventing 'leftover women' being matched with a potential suitor. This kind of extensive and colourful labelling makes the 'leftover' phenomenon almost akin to a market process: men and women of suitable age need to both advertise themselves as well as reevaluate their own purchasing power, in order to achieve what one might call 'targeted marketing'. The desirable strengths on both sides come in the form of a long checklist: for men, it boils down to their breadwinner potential, and for women, many argued, their key desirable factor still lies in their ability to maintain a good household.

These negative stereotypes of gender relations concur with a recent study of 'leftover women' in Shanghai that found that women are not mainly 'leftover' because of their 'unrealisable standards', as argued by the Ministry of Education, but instead of 'discriminatory' and 'controlled' gender restraints (To 2013). The respondents of this sample appeared very aware of these gender restraints: the idea that men preferred women to be 'weaker', or wanted to influence women's choice in their work-family balance. They recognise that an independent and strong woman is unlikely to lower her expectations, whereas the reality maintains that the strengths of these women are actually likely to be undesirable in the eyes of men. Their standards thus remain unrealisable, because they themselves do not realise the true nature of the marriage market. Henceforth, most respondents' advice for these women is still to compromise.

On homosexuality

Although homosexual behaviour was well documented and generally tolerated in ancient China, the pro-Western movement of the late 19th century adopted the then-dominant view in Western psychiatry that homosexuality was a mental illness, a definition that lasted in China until 2001 (Wu 2003). The stigma surrounding homosexuality is not only due to its medical categorisation but also due to the perception that it interfered with the individual's fulfilment of traditional gender roles (Zhou 2006). Indeed, large-scale surveys using representative national samples usually indicate that homosexuality is still, for the most part, rejected by Chinese society. In the World Value Survey of 2007, more than 80 per cent of the respondents claimed that homosexuality is never justifiable, while in the Pew Spring Survey of 2011, only 17 per cent of the respondents thought that homosexuality should be accepted by society. By comparison, the middle class respondents of this sample appeared far more liberal than the national average, where 43 per cent think homosexuality should be accepted by society. Nevertheless, a significant proportion (23 per cent) of the respondents still chose to avoid the question by opting for not sure/prefer not to answer, similar to the Pew survey

(21 per cent of non-answers). This finding suggests that degrees of taboo and ambiguity still persist in Chinese society regarding this topic, which has, in recent decades, been regarded as sensitive.

What is more revealing is that while the survey results suggest a fair degree of tolerance for homosexuality in this sample, the interview data reveal that, in fact, such 'acceptance' comes with terms and conditions. The respondents typically took the meaning of 'acceptance' for a 'lack of hostility', as they did not support the outlawing of homosexuality, nor were they against the idea of universal marriage rights in principle. While attitude towards homosexuality, by way of categorisation, falls under sexual morality, very few thought it was morally deviant on the grounds of its challenge to the traditional gender roles. A considerable number of respondents felt that they could not 'understand' homosexuals, but did not perceive them as 'wrong', simply 'different'. The discussion on homosexuality, while still full of stereotypes, began as a more detached and less accusatory or confrontational one than discussions on the female gender, as most respondents did not think it was relevant to their lives. Unlike the matter of 'leftover women', where most respondents did not hesitate to pass judgement, the issue of homosexuality was seen as 'private' and 'personal', something that 'goes on behind closed doors'. This aversion suggests that the gay community in China is still a largely marginalised group, albeit relatively undisturbed. Indeed, several respondents claimed that they find it hard to accept homosexuality on a personal level, but they are firmly against their discrimination; hence, they would not oppose to 'society's acceptance' of homosexuals in general. Kun cited 'differences in values' as the reason behind his attitude:

> I don't understand gay people. They are like another race entirely. I wouldn't discriminate against them, I think they should enjoy full rights but I probably won't accept them personally. It's to do with traditional values ... if people my age have a hard time accepting them, though we wouldn't bother them, imagine how the elderly must think. Maybe that'd change in the next twenty and thirty years, though.

However, some respondents went on to make differentiations between those they saw as 'genetically gay' and those they saw as 'fashionably gay'. The former 'could not be changed'; hence, they should be accepted, for a lack of a better choice. The latter, the respondents argued, should be 'reformed', as they may have adopted 'skewed values' from pop culture and should be discouraged. 'Gay by choice' was seen as an issue of sexual morality and frowned upon, rather than 'gay by birth', which was met with more neutrality.

> If someone is born homosexual – genetically determined, then I think they should be accepted into society and allowed to marry. But, if someone claims to be homosexual just because it's fashionable, to mess around – then that's unacceptable. Sexuality is predetermined, so they should be accepted, but the lack of sexual morals should be frowned upon.
>
> —*William*

Indeed, during the course of the conversation, many respondents expressed that homosexuals should be accepted into society because 'there is nothing you can do to change them'. Phrases such as 'reform', 'cure' were used interchangeably with 'change', as well as the use of 'normal sexual orientation' instead of 'heterosexuality', indicating that homosexuality was still perceived as abnormal and deviant. The argument for such abnormality is still largely concerned with the reproductive – 'practical', as some suggested – purpose of heterosexual unions, although it is often made in a passive, offhand way, with less heat than the 'fashionable gay-by-choice' mentioned previously. In a curious vein of consistency, the respondents' attitude towards homosexuality was in fact very similar to the way they viewed many social phenomena that they thought were unsatisfactory: with acknowledgement, and with disinterest in strong and proactive opinions in the belief that nothing could be done to remedy the situation. Abbey's answer is fairly representative of such views:

> Well, there's no way to cure them, so I don't see how interfering could help. If their sexuality can be corrected, reformed, then it's best for them to follow the mainstream. I mean the main purpose of human sexuality is reproduction, and you can't have kids if you are gay. But if they can't be changed, then there's nothing you can do about it.

Although many = claimed that homosexuals should be granted full rights, further conversation on the topic suggested 'full rights' also came with clarifications. Abbey, for example, thought homosexuals should be allowed to marry, but saw 'no point in it' as she saw marriage as an institution for the legitimisation of reproduction. Rather, her support for full marriage rights for homosexuals is because she does not think there are grounds for stripping them of such rights, although she maintained that marriage is first and foremost a heterosexual institution. More importantly, the majority of respondents held reservations about the rights of homosexual couples to adopt children – a concern which they often raised without prompt. The primary reason behind such concerns is the impact that gay parents would have on the children: many respondents were worried that children are too 'impressionable' and hence would subconsciously follow their parents' example without 'realising that their sexualities might be normal'. William carefully explained that such 'risks' should be eliminated:

> I have to add – I would accept homosexual marriage, but I am opposed to queer couples adopting children. I would worry about the influence on the child, because you don't know whether he or she will turn out to be queer. Most people are still normal in their sexual orientation – if, in their upbringing they are confused by their parents, that'd be terrible. I want to be conservative about this, and mitigate all possible risks.

Some also worried that due to the lack of legal protection and its marginalised status, homosexual couples were less likely to be in a long-term stable relationship beneficial for child growth. Although some younger respondents were able to logically identify that the stability of a family and success of a relationship were not related to the gender of the parents, most respondents felt that extra 'checks' and 'measures' should be instated before gay couples could be qualified to adopt. There were additional concerns as to how the child would be perceived in society with gay parents, whether there might be discrimination from 'others' – similar to the concerns raised about how leftover women would be perceived by those less 'progressive and liberal' in society, as mentioned previously.

> I think [gay couples] should be allowed to adopt only if they are in a long-term relationship, one that is universally accepted like the ones you have in the West. That's okay. But in China, if two guys turn up with a kid in a park, people will look at you funny and possibly discriminate against you. That can't be good for the kid's upbringing.
>
> —*Jessie*

In a classic display of NIMBYism, nearly all of the respondents claimed that if their children were gay, they would try to 'correct' them, 'force them straight', or intervene in some way to 'bring them back to the mainstream'. One male respondent, despite claiming a non-discriminatory attitude, made a firm announcement that he will break his children's legs if they turned out to be gay. Even in less extreme displays of emotion, most of the other respondents claimed that they will try to intervene, unless it proves to be something unchangeable, then they would have no choice but to give up, as expressed below:

> If my children were gay, then I'd object at first, of course, try to persuade them to live a normal life. It's a heterosexual world after all… but I really don't think there's anything to be done, so eventually I'll let them be.
>
> —*Aline*

Again, their concerns for bringing homosexuals back into the mainstream is related less to the moral side of the issue but to the 'practical' side: it is felt that to be gay, i.e. different, was to invite judgement to their lives, hence bringing unnecessary trouble. Here the imagined voice of the collective holds much power and sway over an individual's opinion and behaviour: for these respondents, the concern about how others will perceive them or their children overpowers how they might feel about the issue in principle. Thus, their attitude towards homosexuality ends up very similar to China's official stance towards the gay community: not encouraged, no active discrimination, and not legally protected and upheld either.

On migrant workers

The socioeconomic effect of rural to urban migration in China is a relatively well-studied phenomenon. Restricted in movement, limited in their access to social benefits and disadvantaged in employment negotiations, migrant workers are often

108 *Viewing those below*

seen as 'second class citizens' in market as well as social situations (Chan 2010). Most of these discriminations are attributed to the *hukou* system, which underpins fundamental differences in the population structure of urban and rural residents, especially with the access and quality of education in rural areas, which places rural residents at a pre-market disadvantage before migrating to the cities (Roberts 2002; Démurger *et al.* 2009). Despite their pivotal role in building China's economy, they often receive negative attention in the media as 'dirty, ignorant and lacking in *suzhi*', and face further discrimination among urban residents (Davin 2000). Indeed, when the middle class respondents of this sample were asked to mark their position on whether they think migrant workers in Ningbo should be treated the same as Ningbo's urban residents (Figure 6.1), one being 'they should be treated completely differently' and ten being 'they should be treated completely the same', only half of the respondents leaned towards similar treatment for migrant workers (six to ten on the scale). Approximately 27 per cent thought some kind of differential treatment is needed (one to four on the scale) while 22 per cent were neutral towards the issue (five on the scale). Their attitude towards migrant worker's children appear to be slightly more egalitarian: overall, 80 per cent of all surveyed respondents believe that migrant workers' children should enjoy the same rights as urban residents' children. In both cases, a slightly larger proportion of self-ascribed salaried class members preferred equal treatment of migrant workers and their children compared to their self-ascribed middle class counterparts (54 per cent versus 44 per cent, and 84 per cent versus 74 per cent, respectively).

Initially, the interview data suggest a very strong support for egalitarian treatment towards migrant workers. The respondents were acutely aware of the discrimination faced by migrant workers, and several protested about the term "migrant worker" (*nongmingong*, 农民工, literally: peasant workers), indicating that to label them as such was derogatory. There were calls to abolish the *hukou* system, which corresponds with the respondents' attitudes on *hukou* in general, as they argued that the negative impact of *hukou* affects the rural population the

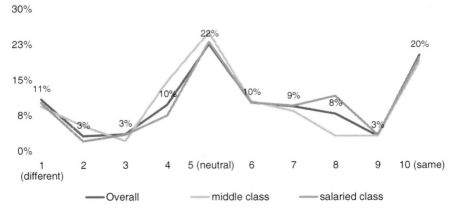

Figure 6.1 Should migrant workers enjoy the same rights and treatment as urban residents in Ningbo? (n=258)

most. Lu's comment was representative of how the urban residents in this sample saw migrant workers: oppressed, and currently treated like second-class.

> They work too hard, and their conditions are pitiful. They do not get recognised enough for what they do. In theory they should be treated equally, but it's hard to actually implement. The *hukou* system we have is a huge impediment. In fact we should abolish the term 'peasant workers' altogether, they are derogatory – not all of them are peasants. Even if they were, why should that separate them from 'urban workers'?

Education is typically seen as the dividing line between the two classes; the regional differences in resource allocation and access to education being one major factor, and *hukou* being the other. In line with the poverty trap argument often made for under-developed countries, some respondents were also aware of the effect of lack of quality education on the children of migrant workers, who will find it difficult to break out of the vicious cycle, as expressed below:

> I think they are so disadvantaged that we should help them. Especially the children of migrant workers – their parents are already suffering this fate, so the state should at least take care of them, to avoid them falling into the same fate as their parents. Why should they take on the worst paid and heaviest jobs? Simply because they only worked the field back home, and had no good education. Even the people in the service sector – their working condition might be better, but they have minimal wage, very little social welfare package, no pension – their outlook is bleak. And all because of no good education.
>
> —*Aline*

In a more chilling vein, Kun underlined migrant worker's second-class status by claiming that their worth as human beings is lower in society's perception. He drew upon frequent news reports of unjust compensations given to migrant workers in the event of an accident in the workplace or on the road, and concluded that migrant workers' inability to defend themselves and their lack of socioeconomic capital define their second-class lives.

> Look, here's how it works nowadays. If a migrant worker gets killed in a car crash, a compensation of ¥600,000 to ¥700,000 can usually settle the case. If a civil servant is killed, the price goes up to 1.5 million. If someone with an American green card gets killed, anything short of 2.5 million and you wouldn't be able to settle. There are prices on human life. That's just how it is. Of course, I feel everyone should be treated the same, but I also know that is impossible.

Again, the respondents' support for equality in principle is marred by their dejected projection that the current situation is unlikely to change. In fact, many recognised that the city's need for migrant workers to take up 'second-class jobs' is what results in their poor working and living conditions, as these jobs are otherwise rejected by urban residents. Unlike city dwellers, they argued, migrant workers' lack of skills and social capital meant they are more likely to accept a trade-off between marginally better pay and poorer working conditions, whereas urban residents such as themselves would consider working conditions to be more, if not most, important. To improve the migrant worker's living standards, in their eyes, changes must be made about their targeted job market; yet, the 'dirty grunt work' is fundamental to a city's function. Jessie remarked that if the migrant workers also reject these jobs, then cities would come to a standstill:

> One of the security guys from my company, a migrant worker, just quit to work on a construction site. The working conditions are horrible compared to what he had in our company but the pay is considerably better. So for them, I think the risks come with the pressure to earn. They are so vulnerable. I think they should be treated better, but who's going to take these dirty jobs then? Come Chinese New Year when every migrant worker goes home, your life just becomes so inconvenient – no one's selling breakfast on the streets, those independent shops are closed, the roads are not swept – you don't really appreciate them until they are gone. You wouldn't want to do these jobs yourselves, but someone's got to. It's a dilemma.

At the same time, the respondents also worried about worsening public security and hygiene in cities, should the migrant worker population become too large. These remarks were often made in an offhand way: one respondent, when commenting on Ningbo's level of social stability, argued that migrant workers were the most prominent agents of instability, but since Ningbo is a receiving rather than a sending city of migrants, Ningbo is deemed more stable as its urban population are not 'floaters'. Furthermore, the respondents often mentioned these concerns as evidence of the migrant workers' poor living standards: it is perceived that because of their low socioeconomic status and high pressure to earn, they are more likely to turn to petty crimes, 'fall in with the wrong crowds', and cause public security concerns. Kosei argued in a somewhat Machiavellian way that migrant workers should be 'rewarded for their city-building effort', and eventually earn their keep:

> I think cities need migrant workers, but too many of them do have a negative impact, especially in terms of hygiene and security. If the city's condition is appealing, more people will flood in and it will become harder to control. But a lot of the urban residents don't want to do the manual labour that migrant workers do, so I think we should have some sort of policy that rewards them with benefit packages according to their work. For example, if they work for x number of years, they can enjoy the same healthcare benefits as urban residents, and y number of years would entitle them to social benefits, etc.

Viewing those below 111

Note that these respondents all claimed that migrant workers *should* be treated the same, yet how they perceived egalitarian treatment should proceed, or if it can proceed at all, is very telling. This contrast illustrates an interesting phenomenon that has been discussed in a previous study looking at urban residents' level of prejudice towards migrant workers: the difference in attitude brought by imagined assimilation or segregation. A study in 2010 found that the respondents with a lower socioeconomic status were more likely to react towards migrant workers in a prejudiced fashion, when considering the migrant worker community in an integrated and assimilated way (Yang *et al*. 2010). When they were asked consider the same community in a marginalised and segregated context, however, their level of prejudice dropped significantly. A similar effect can be observed in this study, if the qualitative data are considered along with the quantitative data – while self-ascribed salaried class respondents appeared to exhibit a more egalitarian attitude in surveys, when they were asked to consider the migrant worker question in an integrated and assimilated context in interviews, their attitudes became less accommodating. The self-ascribed middle class respondents, in contrast, were fairly consistent in their attitudes, suggesting that they had considered the question from all contexts.

The effect of imagined assimilation on the respondents' prejudice becomes more pronounced when the respondents were asked if the children of migrant workers should be allowed to attend the same school as the children of urban residents. Some respondents preferred a segregated schooling system from the beginning, but defended their choices by arguing that it was not an act of discrimination, but necessity: educational resources should be distributed according to children's abilities, so that urban children, with their wider access to private education and resources, could be allowed to flourish rather than being 'dragged down' by migrant children. Ophelia further posited that such segregation would be beneficial for migrant children, too, so that they are not exposed to the high pressure experienced by urban residents, as described below:

> The children of migrant workers should be divided into different classes than the city workers. Not because of discrimination or anything – simply because that they might under-perform compared to their city counterparts, because of their lack of access to extracurricular resources, or the lack of quality basic education from where they came from – they might be discriminated against or bullied if they were put in the same class as the city children. The teachers might get impatient with them, which would hinder their progress further. They might even risk developing a complex or simply turn away from the books. If we put migrant children together, they'd have more in common, and the teachers can do a better job at teaching according to their specific needs.

Meanwhile, several respondents who argued that migrant children should attend the same schools as city children also hesitated when they considered the situation with their own children. In the latter case, the respondents often raised practical concerns, which were previously unmentioned, such as migrant families' inability

112 *Viewing those below*

to contribute towards their children's education and social capital, or the negative influence they might have on city children, in their unsupervised state.

> I personally wouldn't mind if my children went to school with migrant worker's children, that makes no difference in principle. But schools nowadays are so competitive. Everyone wants the best for their children, your classmates and your classmate's parents, they become the earliest social contacts and guanxi that you have. It's that simple. I can understand why people want to segregate the schools. Maybe when I'm actually a dad, I'd realistically pick a school with better human resources, 'purer' students. That's just the human condition.
>
> —*Kun*

> I would on principle agree that my children should be sent to a school where migrant worker's children also attend. But in reality I'd worry about things like what if some of the kids are neglected by their parents, who have to work too hard to keep up with living in the city, that they become sort of 'wild' and be a bad influence on my children. I have to consider that as a parent, so I might choose a more exclusive school for my children after all, just for a peace of mind.
>
> —*Jessie*

Both Kun and Jessie did not shy away from the fact that they would in practice choose an exclusively urban institution for their children, despite their support for egalitarian treatment of migrant workers. This viewpoint is not uncommon: as the topic of discussion became increasingly intimate with their own sphere of social interaction; hence, they became more involved in the decision-making process, the egalitarian principles often gave way to pragmatic concerns. Just as they had acknowledged the difficulties in changing the status quo on many social injustices mentioned previously in this study, they recognise the part they play in upholding existing social prejudices in practice. However, they do not believe this action constitutes active discrimination, but rather compulsion out of lack of choice – they are not prejudiced against the disadvantaged in principle, they argued, but by necessity.

On children's education

The relationship between education and social class is an intricately interwoven one. Not only does education have a direct and recognised impact on one's own socioeconomic status and subjective class identity, it is also a form of inherited capital: the socioeconomic class of the parent has a profound impact on the education experience of the children, which in turn shapes their class position. In her study of American elementary schools, Lareau found that parents of higher socioeconomic status (upper middle class) are more likely to take personal responsibility for their children's education, whether in supplying their children with supplementary education outside of the school or taking close scrutiny over their children's progress in school, whereas working class parents were more likely to hand over such responsibilities to the school teacher (Lareau 2000). Using Bourdieu's theory of cultural capital, it is posited that the socioeconomic class of parents bring different cultural resources and outlooks, which influence their confidence and behaviour in shaping the education of future generations. In other words, the attitude towards children's education could be a significant indicator of the parents' class position, as those with the means and desire to involve in their children's education will do so.

The case of Chinese parents' involvement in their children's education, however, is more contested. On the one hand, cross-cultural analyses have often argued that the Chinese in general adopt a more 'authoritarian' parenting style; hence, they are more invested in their children's education overall (Chao 1996); on the other hand, some research has indicated that there exists a difference in value beliefs and involvement of different socioeconomic groups, whether as a result of rural-urban differences (Chi and Rao 2003), or social class (Louie 2001). To understand where the middle class respondents of this survey stand in these contexts, the respondents were asked to consider two key decisions in shaping their children's education: whether supplementary education will be provided, and whether they will send their children to study abroad.

The answers to both questions, presented in Table 6.2, are overwhelmingly affirmative. Approximately 98% of the respondents answered that they will ask their children to attend extracurricular activities/classes, the majority of whom claimed that they will choose the classes according to their child's interest. Similarly, 94% of the respondents would send their children for education abroad, although most would also prefer that their children return to China after their studies, rather than stay to pursue their careers abroad. Subjective class identity and income bore no correlation in this topic.

The majority of the interviewed respondents appeared to have a strong view about what their children's education will entail and what role they will play in

Table 6.2 Attitude towards children's education (n=258)

Statement	% valid response
Would you ask your children to attend extra tuition classes outside of school?	
Yes, and I will choose the classes for them.	3
Yes, but I will let them choose the classes for themselves.	95
No, I will not ask my children to attend extra classes.	2
Would you send your children abroad for their education?	
Yes, with the prospective of having a career overseas.	39
Yes, with the prospective of having a career back in China.	55
No, I will not send my children overseas for their education.	5

it. If education is a national game, as they believe it is, they realise that their children already have a head start, because of their hard-earned socioeconomic status. However, they also argue that if children were to succeed in parallel comparison with their peers, then 'extra effort' must be put into their curriculum, as well as extracurricular activities. Jane believed this was the norm, as the schools were expecting the parents to provide supplementary education to the students, as expressed below:

> My children would definitely need to go take extracurricular classes. In major cities, kids having two to three extra lessons after school is the norm. I would choose what s/he learns according to what helps him/her the most ... right now school education also focuses a lot on comprehensive *suzhi*, but that also comes in checklists and ticked boxes. Can your children draw? Can she play an instrument? It would be too idealistic to let them grow freely.

Similarly, Ophelia expressed a concern that if she did not provide supplementary education for her children, they would automatically 'lose out' in comparison with their peers. It appears her decision is made out of anxiety and as a reaction to what she perceives to be the educational norm in China, rather than out of any personal beliefs about the value of additional tuition classes outside of schools. The vague sense of distrust of the official education system corresponds with Lareau's study in America, which found that middle class parents feel more comfortable challenging educational authorities because of their own higher educational level. In this case, the respondents' distrust is less due to the material that is taught in schools, but more because of the inability of schools to deal with the sheer number of pupils. Instead of delegating the task to educational institutions, they believe that the norm for someone with their socioeconomic status is to rectify the inadequacies in the official school system by providing supplementary education using their socioeconomic and cultural capital. The need for extracurricular lessons, therefore, is the middle class' practical answer to what they perceive to be an unsatisfactory education system, as described below:

> I think extracurricular classes are needed. If you don't, and your child ends up looking around and realising that everyone can do this puzzle while he can't, it will undermine him. It's best to be prepared. Education in school nowadays is very self-reliant anyway, teachers will think, 'that's all I'm saying on the matter, it's up to you whether you actually understand the material.' So, students have no choice but to take extra classes to keep up with the pace. Studying abroad may mean that the teacher student ratio might be 1:10, but here it's 1:60. There's really no way around it.
>
> —*Ophelia*

All of the interviewed respondents indicated that they would send their children to study abroad, and most seemed confident in their ability to do so. The emphasis, however, was placed on *when* to send their children abroad, rather than *whether* or *where* – many warned against sending their children too early, in fear of letting them 'fall off the wagon'. Being close to the parent and in China's familiar environment should help them establish a moral guide of right and wrong, which could be challenged by the culture shock of studying abroad. The desire to 'shape' their children before allowing them to experience wider horizons is quite common, as expressed below:

> I'd want my children to go abroad, no doubt. To see the world, to develop a good set of values. I'd let them go after high school or university in China. You can't let them go out too young, they don't have the means to filter information yet – I want them to learn from the good of the West, not the drivels of it.
>
> —*Kun*

Another consideration for not exposing their children to foreign cultures too early stems from the need for their children to be 'firmly rooted in the Chinese tradition' first. Not only are Chinese language, culture and traditions perceived as harder to learn but the attainment of 'Chineseness' is almost considered primordial: if one fails to grasp what it means to be Chinese by the time he leaves China, he cannot relearn it upon return, since foreign exposure would have made him an outsider. It is necessary, therefore, for children to establish themselves as Chinese before foreign cultures are introduced to broaden their horizons. Jane explained:

> Studying abroad is a must; going out into the world is very crucial for personal growth … But I don't want him to go too young – I think it's easier for his personal development if he can grow up using his mother tongue and in a familiar cultural environment. If you send him away too early, he'll have a gap [in his identity] between himself and China, and that gap is very difficult to overcome – the longer you leave it, the harder it is to bridge. You go abroad for ten years, who will remember you? You would become strangers with your motherland.

What being 'Chinese' means circles back to the questions of Chinese values discussed in previous chapters, and is often vague and muddied in the respondents' answers. While the elder respondents and those without experience living abroad were usually more concerned about the loss of Chinese values should children be sent out too young, or the risk of being 'steered off course' in the event of cultural shock, the younger respondents and those with study abroad experience were more anxious about their children's cultural identity. This sentiment of being Chinese with cultural values is deeply rooted in their personal experience: respondents like Jane have expressed the struggle to regain their sense of belonging in their time abroad, and hoped to spare their children similar anxieties in the future. Whether their children return to work in China was secondary to those concerns, although it was implied that they will find reintegration into China easier if they are firmly established in their Chinese roots in the first place.

Although the respondents often stressed the importance of their child's comprehensive development and freedom of growth, their vision is still embedded with a keen sense of pragmatism. Providing supplementary education was seen as a means rather than an end in itself, as was studying abroad. Several self-ascribed salaried class respondents, moreover, indicated that they would not encourage their children to go for graduate studies, since they saw no need for further education: the present day job market, they argued, is saturated with highly educated graduates, and experience and social networking in the real world would provide more gains than education itself.

> If I have children, I think all they need is an undergraduate degree. That's the hardline limit nowadays to get a job, anything more doesn't make that much of a difference. Whether you succeed or not has more to do with your EQ, your network of *guanxi* rather than your IQ. No point to read further unless you want to get into research.
>
> —Jessie

Even with the self-ascribed middle class, there was an underlying sense of utilitarianism in education. While they suggested that children should be allowed to grow and flourish according to their interests, it was made on the assumption that reasonable financial returns were guaranteed from their choice of study. In this line of thinking, the respondents often made 'subject stereotypes', where finance, economics and business-related subjects were seen as 'money-maker subjects', in contrast to 'vague, nonspecific [in terms of financial returns]' subjects such as the arts and humanities. The choice is often spoken of in extremely contrasting ends:

> Of course, it's good for you to pursue your passion, but it won't do much good if you starve. With the ever expanding graduate market, getting a job is difficult enough as it is. We might be able to provide our children with a decent education, allowing some choice, but we can't afford to keep providing for him when he graduates. We still need to think practical here. You can't just study something as a hobby – of course, the best case scenario is to have a hobby that pays well, but how likely is that?
>
> —Abbey

Thus, the choices these respondents made were often based on 'making the best of what was available'. Due to their above-average socioeconomic status, the various tools and capitals available to them are already more numerous than most, a fact which they recognise. They also realise that the vast majority of urban dwellers are now in possession of similar capital and resources, and they do not necessarily have any advantage over their peers. There appears to be an implied understanding of how things should work – the idea that there is an operational norm in society that is outside of the official, institutionalised parameters. In a sense, their objective middle class positions allows them to compete on a different level than, say, the rural disadvantaged, but this does not mean the competition is any less fierce. Concessions still must be made, and pragmatism needs to be adopted, to maximise their chance for achieving success and giving their children a real head start.

The Yin and Yang of the Chinese middle class

Consideration of issues of gender, sexuality, attitude towards marginalised groups and investment in children's education, while not class-centric, are nevertheless important in offering valuable insight into how these respondents rationalise and balance the differences between liberal, egalitarian and morally righteous attitudes and pragmatic, prejudiced and amoral concessions to reality. Like many of the topics explored in this book, when the respondents were asked to consider a concept or a question in an abstract, segregated manner, they usually responded with socially desirable answers; however, when they were further questioned and assimilated scenarios were presented, the respondents were equally quickly to turn towards pragmatism and exhibit the same kind of prejudice that they swore they were against. This is not a simple case of hypocrisy: the logic and rationality behind such pragmatic concerns are remarkably consistent, as they constantly tried to balance the 'self' with the 'other', the 'individual' with the 'collective'.

First, the respondents' overall attitude towards gender in this sample is still fairly conservative. The role of women is still primarily considered in the context of marriage and family, and any non-conformative action that does not contribute towards their private lives tends to raise 'practical concerns' on the respondents' part. Yet, these concerns did not stem from any personal traditional or patriarchal views; instead, they are rooted in the firm belief that such traditional and patriarchal views are still the mainstream view in society; hence, it would be unwise to rebel. Here the imagined 'other' is a very powerful critic: much of the respondents' anxiety and reservation in gender issues is a direct result of how they believe others will view their choices, rather than how they view these choices themselves. Thus, in the case of 'leftover women', a distinction was made between those who are too 'picky' and those who 'remain single on principle': the respondents did not object to the latter, but advised the former to be more 'realistic' to avoid the criticisms of the imagined collective. Indeed, the critical voice of the imagined collective almost always drowns out the rationale of the person, as the risk and price of the non-conformative choice are believed to outweigh the benefits.

This line of thinking is carried over to the issue of homosexuality. While the respondents typically had no qualms with the notion of equal gay rights, reservations were made when they considered the question in a more assimilated term – whether gay couples should be allowed to adopt and exert their influence on future generations. Such reservations often turned into objections when they were asked to consider the possibility of their own children being gay, as the decision-making processes required more intimate thinking. It is clear that prejudiced attitudes are still prevalent, although open hostility towards strangers who are gay is less evident, partly because there is the lack of any firm religious beliefs, and partly because homosexual communities are still largely marginalised in China. Again, there is very little moral qualm with the issue, as the respondents did not view homosexuality as 'wrong', simply 'different'. Similar to their attitudes towards 'different kinds of leftover women', distinctions were drawn between those who were seen as gay by choice, and those who were gay by birth – the respondents were generally more tolerant towards the latter, as they believed nothing could be done. This is consistent with the attitudes exhibited in other chapters with social injustices and the condition of socioeconomic institutions: the acceptance of the status quo is generally very high, and the expectation of change where they deem not possible or practical is very low. As such, the respondents often modified their behaviour to suit what they believed was the status quo, to minimise conflict. If there was nothing to be done, then the status quo is simply taken 'as is'.

Similar patterns can be observed in their attitude towards migrant workers. While the respondents acknowledged and understood the disadvantages faced by the migrant worker population, they also recognised the incremental role migrant workers play in the optimal performance of urban cities. It is widely agreed that they should be treated better and remain on equal terms with urban residents, although not many could envisage how an egalitarian attitude could translate to reality. The same is true when they were asked to consider the possibility of a mixed school for migrant children as well as urban children: many agreed to it on principle, but admitted that they will most likely reconsider and send their children to a 'pure' urban establishment in fear of a compromised educational experience. The reasons cited for changes in behaviour are again practical, which is rooted in their belief that they cannot change the external environment; hence, it would be best if individual choices were modified to minimise perceived risks.

Finally, the respondents' strong support for supplementary education and education abroad could be seen as an act of modified behaviour on a personal level, in response to the inadequate educational institutions already in existence. In both cases, utilising their socioeconomic and cultural capital to give their children a head start is seen as the norm, as the respondents were more anxious about the potential consequences in failing to comply with the implied norm. As with all of the issues discussed in this chapter, the urge and tendency to horizontally compare oneself are prevalent. Although the respondents of this study show evidence of individualised thinking, i.e. being able to accept ideas outside of the mainstream norm, their behaviour is still very much based on the context of the collective. Much of the discrepancies in attitude and behaviour are the result of a clash between intrinsic values – which hold less objections – and external realities, which are filled with imagined constraints.

This kind of compromise may be nothing new. As the Chinese historian Ray Huang wrote in *1587: A Year of No Significance*, the Chinese intelligentsia have always struggled between the Yin and the Yang, the selfish desires of the private and the good of the public, pragmatism and idealism. Morals and principles were always socially desirable, but not necessarily achievable, or even practical. Although Huang was writing mainly about the Chinese bureaucrats, the same idea applies here. Well-educated, exposed to Western ideologies and armed with new knowledge and new riches, the Chinese middle class are fully appreciative of the socially desirable liberal and individualistic ideals of the globalised twenty-first century, while remaining conscious of the fact that ideals cannot always be translated straightforwardly into reality. There appears to be a distinct awareness between the difference of 'what should be done' and 'what can be done', as well as 'what should be' and 'what is'. The former represents the Yang, which is publicly declared, socially and morally desirable, but elusive. The latter is the Yin, which is a collective of the private, Machiavellian, and pragmatic; however, it affords them room for manoeuvre and is more tangible. Neither is right or wrong, as Yin and Yang are simply viewed as the natural order of things, 'as is'. The struggle and compromise between the two are often a process of accommodation, where surface attitudes based on detached thinking gives way to reserved, assimilated decisions and finally, privately modified behaviour. For the middle class in the middle kingdom, they seem less inclined to choose one over the other, but are more concerned about finding a balance.

Conclusion
The middle class in the Middle Kingdom

This book set out to investigate three things: who do the (objectively categorised) Chinese middle class think they are, what do they think about a variety of socio-economic and sociopolitical issues, and why do they think the way they do. A synthesised summary of key findings is as follows.

1. Class is defined by exclusion as much as, if not more than, inclusion

At first glance, the respondents' understanding of social stratification and their class identity is underlined by contradictions. There is an overwhelming consensus that stratification exists in Chinese society, yet just over 50 per cent of all of the respondents felt certain that they belonged to a specific class or strata. Nearly all of the respondents fall into the objective middle class category, yet little under half would identify themselves as such. When considered together, however, these contradictions underscore a key point in the social construction of class: that people are more confident of class *differences* than they are of class *similarities*. More often than not, the respondents' class identities are defined by exclusion rather than inclusion, in that they find it easier to discard *unfitting* class labels ('I do not have other sources of income outside my working wage; hence, I am not middle class') than adopting *befitting* labels ('I earn more than x amount; therefore, I am middle class'). This tendency is true both in their subjective perception and in their lifestyle habits: what defines middle class and salaried class is not where they both shop or eat, as there are significant overlaps, but in activities and establishments that they do *not* participate in or visit. The fact that the method of elimination and exclusion is more powerful in defining both class identity and class *habitus* suggests that while class-based social comparison is commonplace, class-based social cohesion is still lacking.

2. Being middle class is more than being 'middle income'

Despite a lack of positive identification with any class identity labels, there appears to be a general consensus among the respondents that being middle class is more than just having a certain amount of money. Income is, of course, an essential prerequisite; often, the respondents' imagined middle class income is several times, even ten times, more than the scholarly definition. The emphasis is not whether an individual's income is considered 'middle', but rather if his income can afford him a 'middle lifestyle', free from material anxieties, with 'enough to spare'. It is the concept of 'spare money', which is relative rather than absolute and which underlines someone's middle class position. Only those with money to spare can pursue the cultured aspect of middle class experience, which is distilled in their *suzhi*, an aggregation of beliefs, attitude and behaviour. These two aspects are seen as interrelated and dependent on one another: without adequate income, the cultivation of culture is very difficult, and without culture, riches alone only makes a parvenu. In acquiring the middle class label, income is simply the entry requirement; one cannot hope to graduate as middle class without passing as 'cultured' and 'with *suzhi*' in the eyes of the beholder.

3. Subjective class identity influences lifestyle and consumption patterns, but has less bearing on values and sociopolitical attitudes

Since class position is perceived to be dependent on both income and 'culture', the easier and simplest way of discerning these hard and soft indicators are by observing one's lifestyle choices and consumption patterns: after all, the main determinant behind one's lifestyle is his income and how he spends that income. Through similar processes of exclusion, the subjectively salaried class and the subjectively middle class occupy two overlapping but distinct *habitus* in the same objective middle class category. Without 'extra income to spare', the self-identified salaried class are more anxious in life, less content about their standards of living, less likely to visit high-end or luxurious shopping establishments and prefer popular entertainment over high culture alternatives. Their middle class counterparts have more room for manoeuvre and stress their ability to choose a comfortable and high-cultured lifestyle, although they might also prefer to live economically in their day-to-day life.

Nevertheless, these identity-based distinctions do not carry over strongly to the respondents' sociopolitical attitudes, values, or behaviour. For the respondents, class identity is more about the private than the public: how a person behaves as an individual, rather than how he relates to society. Subjective class identity did not produce a consistent line of thinking with regard to the latter; the self-identified salaried class and middle class might disagree over any number of single issues, but they do not occupy different ends of the political spectrum, or indeed have a coherent political position at all. This suggests that even if the Chinese middle class could be considered as a class, it is at best a class 'category', rather than a class 'group', the former of which only provides a potential basis for the latter. If one subscribes to E. P. Thompson's concept of class as a 'happening' rather than a social construct, then the Chinese middle class in its sociopolitical form has yet to 'happen'.

4. Chinese Communist Party (CCP) membership still has a significant influence on middle class attitudes and behaviour

In key areas such as the respondents' sociopolitical attitudes and assessment of the role of the state, CCP membership and state employment status often had a more significant bearing on middle class attitudes than their subjective class identity or income. The influence is likely to be a subconscious one, however, as no respondents made references to their CCP membership or employment within the state apparatus when explaining the reasons behind their attitudes. As expected, a larger proportion of CCP members and state employees exhibited politically conservative attitudes; they generally find society to be fairer, are more likely to look towards the government as a patriarchal leader and are less likely to participate in politics outside of an official capacity. It is not clear, however, whether their relatively meeker attitudes are due to their party affiliations or whether they joined the party because of their conformative nature. Either way, affiliations with the party and the state are still a significant influencing factor on peoples' attitudes and behaviour, one that moves beyond simple ideological discourse. Aside from physical participation in protests, there is little evidence that they exhibit conservative attitudes out of fear: it seems much more likely that they still hold the *competency* of the party and the state in high regard; thus, they would not and do not see the need to challenge it.

5. The Chinese middle class may be receptive to global ideas, but remain largely Chinese in their values

Although the values debate produced conflicting and varying answers, when viewed overall, it does appear that the Chinese middle class are more Chinese in their value identification than otherwise. The reason for this is severalfold: first, the majority of the respondents expressed a greater affinity with Chinese values, despite their inability to pinpoint what these values are, suggesting an inherent preference for tradition. Second, the respondents appeared to have a clearer understanding of universal values and the institutions that they represent, yet their appreciation of its merits did not warrant a subjective departure from their Chinese value identities. Indeed, this sample of middle class respondents in general did not think liberal democratic institutions based on Western universal values should be welcomed in China without reserve or modification. Third, although the respondents' understanding of Chinese values was vague and imprecise, it is in fact reflective of the interwoven nature of China's principal schools of thought: Confucianism, Taoism and, to an extent, Buddhism. Throughout the study, references were drawn to Confucian ethics, morality, preference for social order and Taoist concepts of harmony and inaction, suggesting a deep embedding of these ideas in everyday life, even if their usage is unqualified. On a few occasions where ideas with a more Western influence were used, such as 'rights', it is still mentioned within a traditional framework, such as a paternalistic government. Indeed, universal values are not seen as mutually exclusive to

Chinese values; instead, both sets of value systems are recognised to have their own merits and failings and are urged to learn from each other.

6. Privatisation is welcomed as an addition to state-owned public institutions, rather than its replacement

Despite high levels of dissatisfaction with the current state-owned public services, such as healthcare and education, these middle class respondents do not favour privatisation as a remedy to the problem. Private alternatives as an addition to the existing system are welcomed, but privatisation of existing institutions is vehemently opposed by the middle class respondents because they believe the current unsatisfactory state of public affairs is largely due to China's overpopulation and inequality in resource distribution, both of which are results of complex factors, often outside of state control. Thus, the private sector is seen as a means to alleviate pressure on the state, by allowing the rich a market choice, rather than an end to replace state involvement in the public sector. The state as an impartial, non-profit driven vessel for upholding the 'greater good' (i.e. social security) must be preserved, and reform should be aimed at improvement, rather than a complete overhaul.

7. Like a good parent, the state should provide macro-level management to facilitate micro-level freedom and self-reliance

The middle class ideal of the state is not unlike an ideal Chinese parent. The state is expected to take care of its citizens in areas where they have little control over (healthcare and macroeconomic interventions), while allowing a degree of freedom for the citizens to manoeuvre within a legal set of parameters erected to ensure social order and stability. Just like a busy parent, the state is not omnipotent, and cannot be expected to take care of everything: therefore, where the individuals are capable, they are expected to be self-reliant. In the case of the middle class, they are able to offset state ineffectualness in areas of pension and education by opting for the private solution, but they also recognise the inability of the disadvantaged to do so. Thus, the state is expected to improve the safety net it provides for its disadvantaged citizens, while leaving free the areas and the people who are doing well for themselves.

8. The sociopolitical attitudes of the middle class should be analysed within the context of their understanding and expectations of the state

In the surveys, the middle class sample of this study exhibit similar pro-liberty and pro-egalitarian attitudes to other big data set surveys such as Pew Global surveys. The interview data, however, reveal that the recognition of political liberty and social justice in principle do not necessarily translate into any behavioural changes, or indeed result in any pro-reform attitudes. The reason for this is again severalfold.

8.1 The social gentleman's agreement

In line with the Confucian tradition, the concept of 'rights' is still weak among the middle class, and the relationship between the state and the citizen is not so much a social contract, but a social gentleman's agreement. Their support for democratic notions bears more resemblance to Mencius' idea of people-based governance, where the government derives its legitimacy from being able to deduce and satisfy the people's needs. The emphasis here is government performance, rather than representativeness, so that the people do not and need not see themselves as a separate political entity, either in parallel to or opposite of the state. Thus, the people may be supportive of reform, but it will always remain an initiative of the state.

8.2 Empathy towards the limits of government

These middle class respondents have a certain amount of awareness and empathy towards the limits of government, so their expectations towards government accountability and executive capacity are largely managed. As mentioned before, the state is not seen as omnipotent, and many factors influencing social injustice are seen as outside of the state's control. Once it is established that external factors such as overpopulation and 'morality' are as much to blame as internal factors such as corruption and nepotism, state effort in negating either aspect is more easily appreciated.

8.3 Change requires collective effort

By acknowledging that both external and internal factors are responsible for shaping the sociopolitical realities of China, these middle class respondents also recognise the need for the state and the people to work in tandem. Individual action is seen as unhelpful because the main causal factor of injustice and by extension the main agents needed for change lie not with the individual, but with the collective.

8.4 The historical legacy of the Confucian social order and the socialist state

China's particular historical legacy and development trajectory have inevitably altered the people's perception of the state and its sphere of responsibility. Whereas in the West, the state has expanded from the classical liberal idea of 'leave the drunkard in the gutter' to the modern welfare state, the Chinese state has retreated from its all-encompassing socialist days: in a sense, these middle class respondents are very aware that their present socioeconomic well-being is the result of that trade-off between individual freedom, which comes with risks, and egalitarian security, which is stifling. As beneficiaries of the post 1980s reform, middle class expectations towards the Chinese state remain largely economic, which by virtue of their current socioeconomic position have been met.

8.5 Watchful observers?

Thus, in a wider debate of whether the Chinese middle class will be social stabilisers or agents of democratic change, it is perhaps more appropriate to describe them as 'watchful observers'. Familiar with Western ideals but immersed in Chinese culture, they are neither blind followers of the state nor its decided opposition. As with their political class identity, the sociopolitical role of the Chinese middle class has yet to happen; its emergence is likely dependent on the complex interactions between their expectations towards the state and how the state chooses to respond to them.

9. Middle class discontent is offset by the acknowledgement that they are also 'middle' in the food chain

As their 'middle' label is adopted via a method of elimination, the respondents inevitably recognise that they, by their definition of middle, are neither the powerful elite nor the disadvantaged. While they too experience the injustice and inequality in society, they are able to situate themselves in comparative context: horizontally, they already fare better than those in the poorer regions of China; longitudinally, they have been allowed more success and socioeconomic advancement than their parents and grandparents. Again, there is a sense of a trade-off, the idea that true egalitarianism would not have allowed the middling position that they enjoy now. It appears that these middle class respondents are cognisant of the fact that they, by virtue, have to occupy the position in the food chain where they are both 'exploited' by those above, and 'exploitative' of those below. Such class positions are not understood in a militant or conflictory context, rather it is regarded 'as is'. Thus, the effect of this knowledge negates, rather than exacerbates, social conflict, as they are neither in explicit opposition, nor allegiance, to any particular social group or political entity.

10. Middle class nationalism is influenced both by their endogenous view of the 'self' and the exogenous view of the 'other'

On the one hand, the middle class sample of this study appear to be less nationalistic than the national average found in global surveys; they are appreciative of certain strengths in Western societies and are aware of the equivalent shortcomings in China. On the other hand, they still exhibit relatively strong defensive and contrarian attitudes when considering foreign powers, and even belligerent attitudes towards some smaller neighbouring nations. These complex attitudes again require careful unpacking.

10.1 Nationalism, not national supremacy

First, it must be emphasised that very few middle class respondents felt Chinese culture was superior to others or that it is in nature beneath others. Their exposure to foreign values and information seem to have a mitigating effect on any extreme tendency to 'lean towards one side', in that they are neither convinced of China's cultural supremacy nor the West's. The result is that they appear to appreciate the strengths and shortcomings of both cultural systems and would not advocate the domination of one set of values and practices over the other.

10.2 Defensive and reactive, not propagative and proactive

Congruent with numerous studies on Chinese nationalism as a whole, the nationalistic sentiments of the middle class respondents in this study also have strong defensive and reactive elements. In fact, the defining characteristics of China's foreign policy are seen as defensive and reactive, as opposed to America, whose global hegemony is seen as associated with the imposition and exportation of their values. Contrastingly, the respondents are both confident in China's ability to rise and defend herself as a powerful nation, while remaining adamant that she will not provoke or impose her strength upon others. This was particularly relevant when the respondents were asked to consider Japan, as many emphasised that they did not want war, but would not be afraid to rise to the challenge, if provoked. This ability to 'rise to the challenge' is what underlines their national pride, as they view China's 'century of humiliation' with a strong sense of victimisation, and they believe that China has since strengthened its socioeconomic and military prowess.

10.3 Japan: dangerous in its admirable culture

Of all the countries included in the survey, Japan received by far the most hostility. There is a noticeable feeling of victimisation and anger towards Japan due to its historical involvement with China, but more importantly, the respondents were able to recognise Japan's culture of efficiency and discipline, which they deemed particularly dangerous, if it was to be applied to Japan's military imperialism. A clear distinction is drawn between Japanese culture and Japanese politics: the former is met with reluctant admiration, the latter universal distaste. This animosity does not necessarily translate into belligerence, however. Diplomatic resolution is still preferred first and foremost in the Diaoyu conflict, although many felt that the current approach is too 'soft'; despite grievances towards Japan's provocations, there is still a general aversion to war. Most respondents are reasonably well informed on this topic and advised caution and wary watchfulness; very few advocated or indeed participated in any extreme forms of emotional outlet, such as boycotting of Japanese goods or anti-Japanese protests.

10.4 America: an imposing leader

The respondents were noticeably friendlier towards America, which many believed deserved its title as leader of the developed world. Despite years of socialist propaganda, there is considerably less political grievance against America, replaced by admiration of its socioeconomic and technological advancement. They were, however, disapproving of America's value exportation, its uninvited imposition of democracy and 'freedom' upon other nations. Whereas learning from Japan's culture was 'learn from thy enemy', selective incorporation of American values was seen to be helpful to China's development as a whole. The emphasis was that they wished to choose which aspects of American culture they wanted to adopt, not unreservedly receptive as a whole; particular stress was given to the fact that democracy should not be imported as a quick-fix for any country, much less through so-called liberating wars.

10.5 The non-superpowers: prejudiced stereotypes

Contrastingly, the reasonably rational and informed attitudes of reluctant respect are not afforded in the case of other non-superpower nations, such as India, the Philippines and North Korea, where the lack of information and interest have led to a noticeably more narrow-minded and prejudiced view among the respondents. Here their answer falls into stereotypes: India was seen as unhygienic and unsafe; North Korea a state of revolutionary ridicule not unlike the Cultural Revolution; the Philippines a 'hoodlum' who keeps 'pestering' China's borders. Unlike the somber remarks given in previous sections, attitudes towards these nations are often flippant and dismissive, it is clear that the respondents do not consider these nations on a par with Japan or America, with which China has a real chance of military conflict. This irreverent, and sometimes even contemptuous, disregard for smaller nations warrants further investigation, as it runs counter to the respondents' proclaimed lack of national and ethnic supremacy.

11. The middle class is very aware of what should be done, what could be done and what is

Middle class attitudes toward marginalised social groups are particularly enlightening on explaining the seemingly inherent contradictions in their attitudes and behaviour, as demonstrated throughout the book. Whereas on an abstract, conceptual level, these middle class respondents are willing to accept social egalitarianism and justice, where their private interests are concerned, they are more likely to react according to pragmatism rather than principle. The contradictions in response are due to the differences in segregated and assimilated thinking: the former is socially desirable and morally straightforward, but exists largely in theory, while the latter is self-centred and occasionally morally ambiguous, but more practical. Thus, these middle class respondents can be at once supportive of equality in the treatment of migrant workers, and reluctant to allow their children to attend the same school as migrant children, or they might accept homosexuality as a social phenomenon, but elect to try and 'cure' their children should they turn out to be gay. There is a constant negotiation between the individual and the collective, between principle and pragmatism, difference and conformity. Thus, the contradictions presented in their attitudes are in fact different layers of reasoning, the result of an intertwining space of what should be done, what could be done and what is. This process inadvertently demonstrates their namesake: the middle class are at their most 'middle' in their struggle to find an equitable balance.

The 'Chinese', the 'middle' or the 'class'?

As stated from the beginning, this book is, at its core, more about the 'middle' in the middle class, rather than the 'class'. While one cannot begin to study the middle class without first considering the rich and often meandering intellectual debate on class itself, one inevitably runs the risk of becoming entrapped in such debates, if one chooses to analyse the middle class (or any class for that matter) in a purely class-central framework. To attempt to understand society and history using a common framework is one thing; to attempt to understand a group of individual who may or may not fit within such framework, and the implication of their presence, is quite another. While the 'death of class' debate has weakened the functionality and, to an extent, credibility of class as an analytical framework, the people within certain class groups have not disappeared – their presence and significance do not dissipate simply because a previously used analytical label has been discarded by their academic observers. Even if we cast aside the intellectually burdened usage of class, it is undeniable that class, like race, ethnicity, gender or sexuality, is at its core a form of identity, which is both derived from, and an active influence on, human attitude and behaviour. Thus, to understand a particular social group that could, and perhaps once had, fit under the label of class, it is ultimately an exercise in understanding how they see themselves, and what their attitudes and behaviour say about themselves.

Ironically, the academic debate on identity is also a historically and intellectually burdened one. From the primordial concept of 'fixed identity' based on pseudo-biology and a checklist of traits, to instrumental and situational concepts of 'fluid identity' dependent on circumstance and cognitive perception, multiple disciplines within the humanities and social sciences have yet to reach a satisfactory conclusion on what identity consists of, and how identity itself can be identified. The general consensus, without getting too deeply involved in the debate itself, however, is that identity is multi-faceted and flexible; it is multi-layered, some of it we are born with, and some of it we choose to adopt later and at specific times. The identity of self is not singular, nor is it exclusive to one set of labels: depending on internal experience and external stimuli, one set of identity might supersede the other, resulting in different actions under different circumstances. Thus, when contemporary commentators are talking about the Chinese middle class, we should ask: are we more concerned about the 'Chinese', or the 'middle class'?

The answer is, of course, dependent on the interest of the observer. For those who are keen to utilise the vast market the newly affluent will create in China, they are no doubt more interested in the 'middle class' aspect of this social group, which denotes both a good income and a desire to spend. For those who are attentive towards the potential sociopolitical impact of middle class in China, they cannot simply overlook the fact that the identity of this social group is influenced as much by China's historical and cultural legacy as their socioeconomic position. Thus, different focal points to the debate have generated different results: some argue that the Chinese middle class will act according to its class category, while others make a case for Chinese exceptionalism due to their unique cultural and national characteristics. The reality, however, is more complicated: just identity as a concept is dependent on both the ego and the alter ego; the Chinese middle class is perhaps best understood in relative rather than absolute terms. When viewed within the context of the 'global middle class', they appear to be more prominently Chinese; when viewed within the context of Chinese society, they are undeniably middle class in comparison to their counterparts with different socioeconomic statuses. Thus, the significance of the Chinese middle class as a social group, presence and phenomenon is also dependent on the circumstance and context in which they are being considered.

If one reads Fei Xiaotong's *From the Soil: The Foundations of Chinese Society* with the middle class in mind, one would find that the rural peasants of China and the urban middle class are at their very core, not very different. Yes, their consumption habits are wildly dissimilar, and their differing levels of education precipitate the differences in their opinion, but in their core they are both bound by the same thing: the social structure in which they find their place and their purpose. A middle class person might exhibit individualistic tendencies in his behaviour, especially in consumption patterns, but this process of individualisation does not necessarily bleed over to other aspects of his life. As members of the Chinese society, middle class person are, as their non-middle class counterparts, bound by their roles among the collective; yet unlike their rural counterparts, their modern and urban experience dictates that they must negotiate their way between the remainder of the *Gemeinschaft* (organic community) and the emergence of the *Gesellschaft* (contract-based society). Thus, they are also 'middle' in the sense that they occupy the intermediate space between the collective and the individual, the traditional and the modern, the public and the private.

This search for the middle ground is what underlines the numerous contradictions that shape and define the middle class in China today. This is not to say that such contradictions are unique to the middle class – indeed, in Arthur Kleinman's *Deep China*, it is suggested that there are many 'selves' within each Chinese individual. On the one hand, the fast-paced modern lifestyle has encouraged people to interact on an impersonal, individual level, where the idea of 'self' predominates; on the other hand, the self is still reliant on the morals and expectations of the collective and feels certain responsibilities towards it. It is those expectations and responsibilities that create the conflict: in the case of the Chinese middle class, they are both eager to differentiate themselves from the 'plebs' by their superior *suzhi* and values, while at the same time, they only have so much capital that they must focus their resources on protecting their own interests, and the interests of those close to them. What is more confusing is that in both scenarios, they are at once 'selfish' and 'selfless' – to subscribe to egalitarianism and justice is at once 'selfless' in its value and 'self-defining' in the act of choosing such values, while to act in an amoral self-centred way can be at once 'selfish' in its gain and 'selfless' in its motivation. After all, no Chinese individual can claim sole existence outside his kinship network; thus, to protect one's interests is also to protect one's kin. Similar to the choosing of identity labels, the adoption of different 'selves', values and attitudes constitutes a situational and instrumental process, dependent on both internal and external stimuli. In the end, the middle class is both divided and defined by its contradictions – their pursuit of the 'self', the private and the different, is constantly overshadowed by the pull of the collective, the public and the other.

This struggle is particularly significant because it is both old and new. Historically, the Confucian social order has always ascribed a responsibility to the 'learned', the 'gentlemen', the intelligentsia, to lead the under-educated plebs. The people who would have fulfilled these traditional guiding roles in society are, by and large, what we would call 'middle class' today. Indeed, we have seen that much of their social identity is dependent on separating themselves from the qualities that they deem unfit for their middle class label. On the one hand, they are deeply influenced by the traditional Confucian-Taoist Chinese values, which place the harmony of a hierarchical social order and moral upstandingness above all else; on the other hand, they are heavily exposed to Western ideas of competition, individualisation and 'everyman for himself', which denounces the validity of Confucian virtues. If the middle class are to have an avant-garde consciousness and a leading role in society, then, which set of values should they uphold? Whether they take the role of social stabilisers or whether they become agents of democratic change is, in fact, both within the purview of their 'leading role' in society. The difference simply lies in the way they, and we as observers, interpret the definition of these roles. If we consider their insistence, as demonstrated in this study, that Chinese and Western values are compatible, then it is clear that the Chinese middle class may not ascribe to any singular or exclusive definition of their role.

Thus, to invoke a Taoist concept that is deeply intertwined within, and surprisingly representative of, Chinese culture, the Chinese middle class are, at its root, an infusion of Yin and Yang. The significance in this conception is twofold: first, as is well-known, the idea of Yin and Yang is about balance; second, the existence of Yin and Yang is always relative. The latter is particularly important because Yin and Yang, while representing opposing ideas and forces, do not suggest a moral right or wrong; like night and day, their very meaning is dependent on each other. The middle class are more than aware that they were only able to achieve their socioeconomic status by exploiting an individualistic, amoral and competitive environment, which allowed them to accumulate enough capital to set themselves apart from the rest with their superior *suzhi*. To denounce the very path in which they have found their success and their differentiating identity would be hypocritical. Moreover, what Yin and Yang represents could also ostensibly reverse according to circumstance: while normally the support of social justice would be Yang, and the selfish exploitation of *guanxi* networks would be Yin, if the latter is done for the benefit of family and kin, then the selfless motivation of it immediately becomes the Yang, and any obstinate adherence to moral principle would be considered Yin, as it represents the selfish desire to be morally upstanding above all else. Thus, Yin and Yang constitute a reciprocal process, and there is no permanence on the other side. Indeed, the classical representation of the Yin Yang fish in Chinese literature is a revolving one, where the tail and the head of the fish are connected and inseparable from each other. When viewed within this framework, then the contradictions and divisions inherent to the Chinese middle class become its defining characteristic, as their 'middleness' is, at its core, a search for balance.

Imagining the Chinese middle class

Enter the keyword 'Chinese middle class' into Google and you are immediately returned with more than five billion results: the first few pages are populated with articles and reports from influential media sources such as the BBC, *Economist*, *Financial Times* and *The New York Times*. The core of their message seems unanimous: that there is a class of new riches rising in the East, its numbers have never before been seen, and they will shake the global market, if not the global, or at least the regional, order. Yet, there is very little qualification on who the 'middle class' really are, beyond their role as the eager consumer, or the sociopolitically avant-garde. A most popular definition for middle class income is those who earn between $10 and $100 a day – starting at ¥22,630 a year (Kharas and Gertz 2010). One World Bank report even noted that developing nations' middle class income should start at $2 a day, which converts to merely ¥4,533 a year (Donnan, Bland and Burn-Murdoch 2014). While it is true that vast numbers of the Chinese population in its poor rural regions do still fall *under* these income lines, it is difficult to imagine that any Chinese urban residents would regard this level of income as 'middle class', by any means. Indeed, when the Chinese Statistical Bureau set the national middle income line at ¥60,000 (roughly $26 a day), a sound conclusion by scholarly standards, it was met with widespread ridicule and suspicion, often from the very people that would fit under this middle income criterion (Zhang 2005). There is clearly a cognitive discrepancy between who the observers, especially in the West, think the middle class are, and who the Chinese middle class really think they are – yet, this issue is constantly under-addressed in the global media. It is as if the Western observers are drawing an imaginary circle around an expanding proportion of the Chinese population and assigning them the label of the 'rising middle class', while the very people inside the circle would look at these labels and ask, 'Who, me?'

Why then, does this level of cognitive discrepancy exist? Could it simply be that the Western commentators do not understand China's exceptionalism, or that scholarly researchers are so far detached from real life that they can serve no practical purpose? Before the notion of 'middle class' can be dismissed entirely, it is perhaps prudent to consider that this debate may not be entirely new. In the field of social history, especially modern British history, the role of the middle class as a formidable social force has been a topic of fervent debate, and some of the finer points of the argument could prove to be surprisingly helpful in the Chinese case. After all, the very idea of modernisation theory itself is linked to the role of the middle class in the Industrial Revolution and the French Revolution, whereby this social group with surplus riches spearheaded sociopolitical change. The debate, henceforth, was focused on whether the middle class existed at all; as historians coming from different persuasions argued which came first, in order to pinpoint the exact impact of this supposedly crucial social class. For a good while, the debate had been an adversarial one: either social change in Britain occurred before the middle class; thus, class analysis of the two revolutions was defunct, or the middle class occurred before the social change; thus, it was crucial in the revolutionary making.

However, in a book called *Imagining the Middle Class*, historian Dror Wahrman raised an important point about the subtle space that could exist between social *representation* and social *reality* (Wahrman 1995). The main problem of the debate on whether there was indeed a rise of the British middle class, in his view, was the fact that both sides of the camp believed that the rise of a new social *group* equated with the rise of a social *consciousness*. Thus, if evidence is found in support of the formation of a new social class, a new social consciousness is assumed to follow, while the lack of such consciousness must indicate the absence of the social group in the first place. This assumption is most misleading, as a degree of freedom could exist between what society is perceived to be and society really is. The fostering of the British middle class was in fact borne out of an interaction between political discourse and social transformation, as politicians sought to mobilise political support by appealing to the societal 'middle ground', who was seen as distinct from the corrupt landed elites *and* the revolutionary lower classes. Thus, the middle class is as much 'made' as it is 'happened'; the term and concept were utilised and mobilised before the social class came into any conceivable being.

Drawing on this observation of 18th-century Britain, we might consider the middle class phenomenon in China in a new light. First, to what extent will be the Chinese middle class be shaped by its portrayal in Western media? After all, 'agenda-setting' is a well-accepted concept in the field of media studies, whereby mass media may not influence one's decisions, but it can most definitely influence what one is deciding about (McCombs and Shaw 1972). Social and cultural reproduction theory further tells us that consumer tastes and cultural behaviours can be susceptible to media influence and peer pressure, where one learns what it means to be a member of an 'in-group', and seeks to strengthen and reproduce these characteristics in order to preserve one's social identity. Thus, it is not inconceivable that the Chinese middle class will aspire to become the luxury buyers and avant-garde cultural consumers that media portrays them to be, even if many

Conclusion 133

people in this sample have not yet exhibited these characteristics. In the case of symbolic consumption at least, middle class tastes can be 'made', as much as it can 'happen'.

Second, although the Chinese state is not looking to mobilise the middle class in the same way that the politicians may have done in 18th-century Britain, the rhetoric of 'middle class society' is nevertheless a constant presence in state media. The repeated emphasis on middle class as a public discourse leads us to ask the question: what is the Chinese state talking about when it is stressing the need to foster a mature middle class? In some ways, the official rhetoric's stress on middle class *suzhi* and 'spiritual construction' reminds one of the appeal to middle class morality common in 18th-century England. Yet, it is also vastly different. China, as a secular state, lacks any capacity or indeed will to call for citizen's moral upstandingness on religious grounds. The closet ideal to Christian England is Confucian notions of virtue, which the state is using tentatively and sparingly, as the very idea was denounced by the state not fifty years before. The Chinese state has not explained clearly what it wishes for the middle class to achieve: at a glance, it seems the call for a middle class society is a continuation of *xiaokang* society, encouraged mainly on economic terms. While scholars and the public alike argue over the definition of middle class, its political utilisation remains, so far, elusive. Yet, as Wahrman have demonstrated, a 'well defined sociological referent of social terminology' is neither a prerequisite for its meaningful deployment, nor its argumentative impact (Wahrman 1995). Thus, it is possible that the sociopolitical role of the middle class could also be borne out of interaction between the state expectations of the middle class and middle class expectations of the state.

If the narrative of the British middle class was indeed created out of sociopolitical necessity, what does it suggest for today's China? The narrative is certainly already there, so is the new social category by objective identification. The inevitable question of 'will they or won't they' has resulted in an eager anticipation, or worried watchfulness, of middle class-led sociopolitical change. Yet, to simply argue about possible *outcomes* in China's social transformation is to overlook the *process* of transformation, not just on the outside, but on the inside. Any class action, or even any action led by a major social group, rests on the collective consciousness of its members, which is in turn reliant on their collective identity of themselves, and each other. Again, like the Taoist Yin Yang fish, this process of formation, re-evaluation and contextualisation is often an interactive one. It would be inadequate to consider the Chinese middle class as a coherent, consistent and constant state of being, brought into existence by China's economic growth. There is also no direct correlation between their socioeconomic status and any prescribed socio-political characteristics that we have come to associate with the term 'middle class.' The impact of social class, like another social group, is always greater than the sum of all its individual members: they should be considered first and foremost as *people*, rather than numbers and aggregates that could be summarised using a common denominator. Thus, to understand the Chinese middle class is to first and foremost understand individuals who occupy the middling social space between the powerful elite and helpless poor, whose expanding numbers will become a crucial component of China's evolving social structure. They are both shaped by the social 'category' that they fall under, and they shape the social 'group' they have the potential to become. Just as the rise of modern China needs to be understood in the context of the shifting global order and her interactions with the West, so does the rise of the Chinese middle class.

Appendix

1. Normalised index and threshold for determining which factors are relatively significant

$$NI = \frac{\% \text{ of people choosing } x_i}{\text{average } \% \text{ of all } x} \quad (1)$$

where x_i represents surveyed factors, subscript i denotes the item number of a particular factor, NI is normalised index of the prevalence of a particular factor against other competing factors.

$$\text{Cut-off line} = \frac{NI_{peak}}{\sqrt{2}} \quad (2)$$

where NI_{peak} is the highest value among a group of NI and any items on or above the cut-off line are considered important factors.

2. Threshold for determining significant correlation

In order to compare the relative correlation between various factors in relation to a number of statements, the standard deviations of 'agree' and 'disagree' of each statement among various factors in comparison were computed as shown in equation 3. Therefore, a small standard deviation among the responses of a factor towards a statement, illustrates a small correlation between the given factor and the given statement. In other words, no group of respondents sub-categorised under the given factor, demonstrated a particular preference towards the statement.

$$\text{Correlation of a factor and a statement } Cfs = stdev(\% \text{ of agree}, \% \text{ of disagree}) \quad (3)$$

136   *Appendix*

In order to determine the relative statistical significance of the correlations between a multitude of factors and statements, the mean of the correlation of various factors to a statement was determined in equation 4. This illustrates the statistically expected background average of the correlations. The purpose of this is to determine the 'noise floor' of the correlations, in order to prevent false-positive correlations. Any correlation results at or below the mean value *MCfs* implies the correlation is relatively statistically insignificant.

$$\text{Mean correlation of various factors to a statement } MCfs = mean(Cfs_n)$$
$$\text{where } n = 1, 2, .. \text{ m, represent n numbers of factors} \quad (4)$$

Furthermore, the standard deviation of the previously computed standard deviations of *n* number of factors for a statement Cfs_n were computed in equation 5 in order to determine the relative correlation among the correlations.

$$\text{Relative correlation } RCfs = stdev(Cfs_n) \quad (5)$$

Equation 6 then utilises the relative correlation determined from equation 5 and the background average of the correlations from equation 4 to compute a relative threshold. Any correlation between a factor and a statement calculated from equation 3 with values greater than this threshold implies a correlation that is statistically significant in relation to all of the other factors surveyed.

$$\text{Threshold to determine factors with relatively strong correlation} = MCfs + \frac{RCfs}{2} \quad (6)$$

Bibliography

Agger, Ben. 1991. Critical theory, poststructuralism, postmodernism: Their sociological relevance. *Annual Review of Sociology* 17:105–31.
Anagnost, Ann. 2008. From class to social strata: Grasping the social totality in reform-era China. *Third World Quarterly* 29 (3):497–519.
Atkinson, Will. 2012. Class, individualization and late modernity. In *Search of the Reflexive Worker*. Steven Roberts and Will Atkinson. 768–70.
Bai, Li, Chenglin Ma, Shunlong Gong, and Yinsheng Yang. 2007. Food safety assurance systems in China. *Food Control* 18 (5):480–84. doi: http://dx.doi.org/10.1016/j.foodcont.2005.12.005.
Barton, Dominic, Yougang Chen, and Amy Jin. 2013. Mapping China's middle class. *McKinsey Quarterly* 3:54–60.
Beck, Ulrich. 1992. *Risk society: Towards a new modernity*. Vol. 17. London: Sage.
Beck, Ulrich. 2002. Individualization: Institutionalized individualism and its social and political consequences. Vol. 13. London: Sage.
Bennett, Tony, Mike Savage, Elizabeth Bortolaia Silva, Alan Warde, Modesto Gayo-Cal, and David Wright. 2009. *Culture, class, distinction*. New York: Routledge.
Bian, Yanjie. 2002. Chinese social stratification and social mobility. *Annual Review of Sociology* 28:91–116.
Bian, Yanjie, Ronald Breiger, Deborah Davis, and Joseph Galaskiewicz. 2005. Occupation, class, and social networks in urban China. *Social Forces* 83 (4):1443–68.
Bottero, W. 2004. Class identities and the identity of class. *Sociology* 38 (5):985–1003. doi: 10.1177/0038038504047182.
Bourdieu, P. 1984. *Distinction: A social critique of the judgement of taste*. Cambridge, MA: Harvard University Press.
Bourdieu, Pierre. 1999. Cultural reproduction and social reproduction. Modernity: Cultural Modernity 2:351.
Bourdieu, Pierre. 2000. Making the economic habitus Algerian workers revisited. *Ethnography* 1 (1):17–41.
Brook, Timothy, and B. Michael Frolic, eds. 1997. *Civil society in China*. London: M. E. Sharpe.
Bureau, Ningbo Statistical. 2012. *Ningbo statistical yearbook 2012*. Beijing: Statistical Publishing Company of China.
Cartier, Carolyn. 2008. The Shanghai-Hong Kong connection: Fine jewelry consumption and the demand for diamonds. *The New Rich in China*. 187–200.
Chan, Kam Wing. 2010. The household registration system and migrant labor in China: Notes on a debate. *Population and Development Review* 36 (2):357–64.

Chao, Ruth K. 1996. Chinese and European American mothers' beliefs about the role of parenting in children's school success. *Journal of Cross-Cultural Psychology* 27 (4):403–23.

Chen, An. 2002. Capitalist development, entrepreneurial class, and democratization in China. *Political Science Quarterly* 117 (3):401–22.

Chen, J., and C. Lu. 2011. Democratization and the middle class in China: The middle class's attitudes toward democracy. *Political Research Quarterly* 64 (3):705–19. doi: 10.1177/1065912909359162.

Chen, Jie. 2013. *A middle class without democracy: Economic growth and the prospects for democratization in China*. New York: Oxford University Press.

Chen, Minglu. 2015. From economic elites to political elites: private entrepreneurs in the people's political consultative conference. *Journal of Contemporary China* 24 (94):613–27.

Chi, Jin, and Nirmala Rao. 2003. Parental beliefs about school learning and children's educational attainment: evidence from rural China. *Ethos* 31 (3):330–56.

Clark, Gregory. 2014. *The son also rises*. Princeton, NJ: Princeton University Press.

Clunas, Craig. 1991. *Superfluous things: Material culture and social status in early modern China*. Honolulu: University of Hawaii Press.

Coyner, Sandra J. 1977. Class consciousness and consumption: The new middle class during the Weimar Republic. *Journal of Social History* 10 (3):310–31.

Crompton, Rosemary. 2006. Class and family. *The Sociological Review* 54 (4):658–77.

Crompton, Rosemary, and John Scott. 1999. Introduction: The state of class analysis. *The Sociological Review* 47 (S2):1–15.

Davin, Dellia. 2000. Migrants and the media: Concerns about rural migration in the Chinese press. In *Rural labor flows in China*. Loraine A. West and Yaohui Zhao (eds.). Berkeley: Institute of East Asian Studies, University of California, Berkeley.

Davis, Deborah. 2005. Urban consumer culture. *China Quarterly-London* 183:692.

Davis, Deborah, and Feng Wang. 2009. *Creating wealth and poverty in postsocialist China*. Stanford: Stanford University Press.

Davis, Kingsley, and Wilbert E Moore. 1945. Some Principles of Stratification. *American Sociological Review* 10 (2):242–49.

Démurger, Sylvie, Marc Gurgand, Shi Li, and Ximing Yue. 2009. Migrants as second-class workers in urban China? A decomposition analysis. *Journal of Comparative Economics* 37 (4):610–28.

Devine, Fiona. 1998. Class analysis and the stability of class relations. *Sociology* 32 (1):23–42.

Devine, Fiona, and Mike Savage. 1999. Conclusion: renewing class analysis. *The Sociological Review* 47 (S2):184–99.

Dickson, Bruce J. 2010. China's cooperative capitalists: The business end of the middle class. *China's emerging middle class: Beyond economic transformation*. Washington, DC: Brookings Institution Press. 291–309.

Donnan, Shawn, Ben Bland, and John Burn-Murdoch. 2014. A slippery ladder: 2.8bn people on the brink – FT.com. Available online at http://on.ft.com/Q5VaAO (accessed 19 July 2016).

Ehrenreich, Barbara. 1989. *Fear of falling: The inner life of the middle class*. New York: Pantheon Book.

Fairbrother, Gregory P. 2013. The Chinese paternalistic state and moral education. *Citizenship education in China: Preparing citizens for the 'Chinese century'*. Kerry J. Kennedy, Gregory Fairbrother, and Zhenzhou Zhao (eds.). New York: Routledge. 11.

French, Howard W. 2006. In Chinese boomtown, middle class pushes back. *New York Times*. Dec 18 2016 (http://www.nytimes.com/2006/12/18/world/asia/18shenzhen.html).
Friedman, Edward, and Barrett L McCormick. 2015. *What if China doesn't democratize? Implications for war and peace*. New York: Routledge.
Fukuyama, Francis. 2013. China's middle class gets political. *Financial Review*, 17 August 2013. Available online at www.afr.com/news/policy/foreign-affairs/chinas-middle-class-gets-political-20130815-jhajg (accessed 20 June 2014).
Giddens, Anthony, Franciszek Ociepka, and Wiktor Zujewicz. 1973. *The class structure of the advanced societies*. London: Hutchinson.
Goldthorpe, J. H., D. Lockwood, F. Bechhofer, and J. Platt. 1969. *The affluent worker in the class structure*. Vol. 3. London: Cambridge University Press.
Goodman, D. S. G. 2012. The new rich in China: Why there is no new middle class. *Arts: The Journal of the Sydney University Arts Association* 32:13–36.
Goodman, David S. G. 2014a. *Class in contemporary China*. Cambridge; Malden, MA: Polity Press.
Goodman, David S. G. 2014b. Middle class China: Dreams and aspirations. *Journal of Chinese Political Science* 19 (1):49–67.
Goodman, David S. G., and Minglü Chen. 2013. *Middle class China: Identity and behaviour*. Cheltenham, UK: Edward Elgar Publishing.
Guan, Xinping. 2000. Chinas social policy: Reform and development in the context of marketization and globalization. *Social Policy & Administration* 34 (1):115–30.
Guo, Xinghua. 2001. Chenshi jumin xiangdui boduogan de shizheng yanjiu. *Journal of Remin University of China* 3:71–8.
Guo, Yingjie. 2012. Classes without class consciousness and class consciousness without classes: The meaning of class in the People's Republic of China. *Journal of Contemporary China* 21 (77):723–39.
Halskov Hansen, Mette, and Rune Svarverud. 2010. iChina: The rise of the individual in modern Chinese society. Copenhagen: NIAS Press.
Hanser, A. 2010. Uncertainty and the problem of value: Consumers, culture and inequality in urban China. *Journal of Consumer Culture* 10 (3):307–32. doi: 10.1177/1469540510376906.
Hanser, Amy. 2008. Service encounters: Class, gender, and the market for social distinction in urban China. Stanford, CA: Stanford University Press.
Hou, Jing. 2010. Zhuguan jieceng rentong yanjiu zongshu. *Journal of Zhoukou Normal University* (1):100–03.
Hsiao, William C. L. 1995. The Chinese health care system: Lessons for other nations. *Social Science & Medicine* 41 (8):1047–55.
Hsu, Carolyn L. 2007. *Creating market socialism: How ordinary people are shaping class and status in China*. Durham and London: Duke University Press.
Huang, Philip C. C. 1993. Public Sphere/Civil Society in China? The third realm between state and society. *Modern China* 19 (2):216–40.
Huang, Yeqing, Fei Guo, and Yiming Tang. 2010. Hukou status and social exclusion of rural-urban migrants in transitional China. *Journal of Asian Public Policy* 3 (2):172–85. doi: 10.1080/17516234.2010.501160.
Jing, Xu, and Yue Ximing. 2013. Redistributive impacts of the personal income tax in urban China. *Rising inequality in China: Challenges to a harmonious* society. New York: Cambridge University Press. 362.
Johnson, Dale L. 1985. *Middle classes in dependent countries*. Vol. 3. Beverly Hills: Sage Publications, Inc.

Johnston, Alastair Iain. 2004. Chinese middle class attitudes towards international affairs: Nascent liberalization? *The China Quarterly* (179):603–28.
Jones, D. M. and D. Brown. 1994. Singapore and the myth of the liberalizing middle class. *The Pacific Review* 7 (1):79–87.
Kharas, Homi, and Geoffrey Gertz. 2010. *The new global middle class: A cross-over from West to East.* Wolfensohn Center for Development at Brookings. 1–14.
Kleinman, Arthur, Yunxiang Yan, Jing Jun, Sing Lee, and Everett Zhang. 2011. *Deep China: The moral life of the person.* Berkeley and Los Angeles: University of California Press.
Lam, Hon-Ming, Justin Remais, Ming-Chiu Fung, Liqing Xu, and Samuel Sai-Ming Sun. 2013. Food supply and food safety issues in China. *The Lancet* 381 (9882):2044–53. doi: http://dx.doi.org/10.1016/S0140-6736(13)60776-X.
Lange, Hellmuth, and Lars Meier, eds. 2009. *The new middle classes: Globalizing lifestyles, consumerism and environmental concern.* Dordrecht, Netherlands: Springer Science & Business Media.
Lareau, Annette. 2000. *Home advantage: Social class and parental intervention in elementary education.* Lanham, MD: Rowman & Littlefield Publishers.
Larson, Christina. 29 Oct. 2012. Protests in China get a boost from social media. Available online at www.bloomberg.com/news/articles/2012-10-29/protests-in-china-get-a-boost-from-social-media.
Lash, Scott, and John Urry. 1987. *The end of organized capitalism.* Madison: University of Wisconsin Press.
Lei, Guang. 2003. Rural taste, urban fashions: The cultural politics of rural/urban difference in contemporary China. *Positions: East Asia Cultures Critique* 11 (3):613–46.
Li, Cheng. 2010a. *China's emerging middle class: Beyond economic transformation.* Washington, DC: Brookings Institution Press.
Li, Chunling. 2005. Shehuijieceng de shenfenrentong. *Jiangsu Social Sciences* (6):108–12.
Li, Chunling. 2009. *Formation of middle class in comparative perspective: Process, influence and socioeconomic consequences.* Beijing: Social Science Academic Press.
Li, Chunling. 2010b. Characterizing China's middle class: Heterogeneous composition and multiple identities. *China's emerging middle class. Beyond economic transformation.* Washington, DC: Brookings Institution Press.
Li, Chunling. 2013. Sociopolitical attitude of the middle class and the implications for political transition. *Middle class China: Identity and behaviour.* 12–33.
Li, Fengliang, Mengying Zhou, and Baolong Fan. 2014. Can distance education increase educational equality? Evidence from the expansion of Chinese higher education. *Studies in Higher Education* 39 (10):1811–22.
Li, Guorong. 2008a. Shilun woguo xianjieduan siyin qiyezhu jiecengde shehuishuxing. *Studies in Socialism with Chinese Characteristics* (6):83–7. Available online at www.hprc.org.cn/pdf/SPEC200806019.pdf.
Li, Lulu. 2008b. The social function of the middle class: The new question-oriented approach and multidimensional analysis framework. *Journal of Renmin University* 4 (April 2008):125–35.
Li, Peilin, Guangjin Chen, Yi Zhang, and Wei Li. 2008. Zhongguo shehui hexie wending baogao. *Report on China's Social Harmony and Stability.* Beijing: Shehuikexue wenxian chubanshe.
Li, Peilin, and Yi Zhang. 2008a. The scope, identity, and social attitudes of the middle class in China. *Society* 2:1–19.
Li, Peilin, and Yi Zhang. 2008b. The scope, identity, and social attitudes of the middle class in China. *Society* 2:1–19.

Li, Qiang. 2008c. Gaige kaifang sanshinianlai zhongguo shehui fenceng jiegoude bianqian. *Beijing Social Sciences* 5:47–60.
Ling, Lily HM, and Chih-yu Shih. 1998. Confucianism with a liberal face: The meaning of democratic politics in postcolonial Taiwan. *The Review of politics* 60 (1):55–82.
Lipset, S. M. 1959. Some social requisites of democracy: Economic development and political legitimacy. *The American Political Science Review* 53 (1):69–105.
Liu, Xin. 2001. Zhuanxingqi zhongguo dalu chenshi juminde jieceng yishi. *Sociological Studies* (3):8–17.
Liu, Yuanli. 2004. China's public health-care system: Facing the challenges. *Bulletin of the World Health Organization* 82 (7):532–8.
Logan, Justin. 2013. China, America, and the pivot to Asia. Cato Institute Policy Analysis 717. Available online at http://papers.ssrn.com/sol3/papers.cfm?abstract_id=2228171.
Louie, Vivian. 2001. Parents' aspirations and investment: The role of social class in the educational experiences of 1.5- and second-generation Chinese Americans. *Harvard Educational Review* 71 (3):438–75.
Lu, Hanlong. 2010. The Chinese middle class and Xiaokang society. *China's emerging middle* class. *Beyond economic transformation*. Washington, DC: Brooking Institution Press. 104–31.
Lu, Peng. 2016. Transformation of China's socialist brick: Reproduction and circulation of ordinary cadres. *Handbook on class and social stratification in* China. Cheltenham, UK: Edward Elgar. 279.
Lu, Xueyi. 2002. Research report on social stratification in contemporary China. *Beijing, China: Social Sciences Documentation Publishing House (in Chinese)*.
Ma, Jin, Mingshan Lu, and Hude Quan. 2008. From a national, centrally planned health system to a system based on the market: lessons from China. *Health Affairs* 27 (4):937–48.
Marshall, Gordon. 1997. Repositioning class: Social inequality in industrial societies. London: Sage.
Marx, Karl. 2008. The formation of classes ... (With Engels) (1845–6). In *Cohen, Ira J. Marx and Modernity: key readings and commentary*. Robert Antonio (ed.). Malden, MA: John Wiley & Sons. 2008. 63–4.
McCombs, Maxwell E, and Donald L Shaw. 1972. The agenda-setting function of mass media. *Public Opinion Quarterly* 36 (2):176–87.
Michelson, Ethan, and Sida Liu. 2010. "What do Chinese lawyers want? Political values and legal practice." In *China's Emerging Middle Class: Beyond Economic Transformation*. Li, Cheng (ed). Washington, DC: Brookings Institution. 310–33.
Mills, C Wright. 2002. *White collar: The American middle classes*. New York: Oxford University Press.
Mok, Ka Ho, Yu Cheung Wong, and Xiulan Zhang. 2009. When marketisation and privatisation clash with socialist ideals: Educational inequality in urban China. *International Journal of Educational Development* 29 (5):505–12.
Moloney, Gail, and Iain Walker. 2007. *Social representations and identity: Content, process and power*. New York: Palgrave Macmillan.
Nadeau, Randall L. 2013. *Asian religions: A cultural perspective*. Chichester, UK: John Wiley & Sons.
NHFPC. 2014. National Health and Family Planning Commission of the People's Republic of China. 2014 Work Report on Food Safety Issues in China. Available online at www.nhfpc.gov.cn/sps/s7892/201504/0b5b49026a9f44d794699d84df81a5cc.shtml (accessed 19 February 2016).

Bibliography

Pakulski, Jan, and Malcolm Waters. 1996. The reshaping and dissolution of social class in advanced society. *Theory and Society* 25 (5):667–91.
Paton, Kirsteen. 2014. *Gentrification: A working-class perspective.* London: Ashgate Publishing, Ltd.
Pew, Research Center. 2011. *Pew global attitudes survey in China.* Washington, DC.
Pew, Research Center. 2012. *Pew Global Attitudes Survey in China.* Washington, DC.
Pitsilis, Emmanuel, David A Von Emloh, and Yi Wang. Filling China's pension gap (China research). *The McKinsey Quarterly* 20+. Academic OneFile. Web. 24 July 2016.
Pow, Choon-Piew. 2009. Gated communities in China: Class, privilege and the moral politics of the good life: Oxon, London: Routledge.
Pye, Lucian W. 1991. The state and the individual: An overview interpretation. *The China Quarterly* 127: 443–66.
Qiao, Lijun, and Tianze Chen. 1994. *China cannot afford chaos.* Beijing, China: Chinese Party School Press.
Rawls, John. 1999. *A theory of justice.* Cambridge, MA: Harvard University Press.
Reischauer, Edwin Oldfather, and John King Fairbank. 1960. *East Asia: The great tradition.* Boston: Houghton Mifflin.
Roberts, Kenneth D. 2002. Rural migrants in urban China: Willing workers, invisible residents. *Asia Pacific Business Review* 8 (4):141–58.
Rueschemeyer, Dietrich, Evelyne Huber Stephens, and John D. Stephens. 1992. *Capitalist development and democracy.* Oxford, UK: Polity Press.
Savage, M. 2005. Working-class identities in the 1960s: Revisiting the affluent worker study. *Sociology* 39 (5):929–46. doi: 10.1177/0038038505058373.
Savage, Michael. 2000. *Class analysis and social transformation.* Buckingham: Open University Press.
Savage, Mike. 2003. Review essay: a new class paradigm? *British Journal of Sociology of Education* 24 (4):535–41.
Sennett, Richard. 1972. *The hidden injuries of class.* CUP Archive.
Shambaugh, David L., ed. 2000. *Is China unstable? Assessing the factors.* Armonk and London: M. E. Sharpe.
Skeggs, Beverley. 2004. *Class, self, culture.* London: Cambridge University Press.
Skeggs, Beverley. 2015. Introduction: Stratification or exploitation, domination, dispossession and devaluation? *The Sociological Review* 63 (2):205–22.
Sonoda, S. 2010. Emergence of middle classes in today's urban china: Will they contribute to democratization in China? *International Journal of China Studies* 1 (2):351–69.
Standing, Guy. 2011. *The precariat: The new dangerous class.* London: Bloomsbury.
Sun, Feng, and Jing Jian Xiao. 2012. Perceived social policy fairness and subjective wellbeing: Evidence from China. *Social Indicators Research* 107 (1):171–86. doi: 10.1007/s11205-011-9834-5.
Sun, Wanning, and Yingjie Guo. 2013. *Unequal China: The political economy and cultural politics of inequality.* Netherlands: Springer.
Tajfel, Henri. 2010. *Social identity and intergroup relations.* Vol. 7. Cambridge, UK: Cambridge University Press.
Tang, Beibei, and Jonathan Unger. 2013. The socio-economic status, co-optation and political conservatism of the educational middle class: A case study of university teachers. *Middle Class China: Identity and Behaviour.* Cheltenham: Edward Elgar. 90–109.
Tang, Min. 2011. The political behavior of the Chinese middle class. *Journal of Chinese Political Science* 16 (4):373–87. doi: 10.1007/s11366-011-9166-y.

Bibliography 143

Tang, Min, Dwayne Woods, and Jujun Zhao. 2009. The attitudes of the Chinese middle class towards democracy. *Journal of Chinese Political Science* 14 (1):81–95. doi: 10.1007/s11366-008-9034-6.

Tang, Wenfang, and Benjamin Darr. 2012. Chinese nationalism and its political and social origins. *Journal of Contemporary China* 21 (77):811–26.

Tang, Wenfang, and William L Parish. 2000. *Chinese urban life under reform: The changing social contract*. Cambridge, UK: Cambridge University Press.

Thompson, Edward Palmer. 1963. *The making of the English working class*. Vol. 322. IICA. New York: Random House.

To, Sandy. 2013. Understanding Sheng Nu (Leftover Women): The phenomenon of late marriage among Chinese professional women. *Symbolic Interaction* 36 (1):1–20.

Tomba, L. 2009. Middle classes in China: Force for political change or guarantee of stability? In *PORTAL Journal of Multidisciplinary International Studies* 6 (2). Available online at http://epress.lib.uts. edu.au/journals/index.php/portal/article/view/1026/1507 (accessed 1 September 2015).

Tomba, Luigi. 2004. Creating an urban middle class: Social engineering in Beijing. *The China Journal* 51:1–26.

Tu, Weiming. 2014. Multiple modernities: A preliminary inquiry into the implications of the East Asian modernity. In *Globalistics and globalization studies: Aspects & dimensions of global views*. L. E. Grinin, I. I. Ilyin, A. V. Korotayev, A. D. Ursul, E. Kiss, A. N. Chumakov, O. G. Leonova, Tu, Weiming, P. G. Kirchschlaeger, and A. Howell. Volgograd, Russia: Uchitel Publishing House.

Tyler, Imogen. 2015. Classificatory struggles: Class, culture and inequality in neoliberal times. *The Sociological Review* 63 (2):493–511. doi: 10.1111/1467-954x.12296.

Wahrman, D. 1995. *Imagining the middle class: The political representation of class in Britain, c. 1780–1840*. Cambridge, UK: Cambridge University Press.

Wasserstrom, Jeffrey. 2008. China's middle class rising. *The New York Times*, 21 Jan, 2008. Available online at www.nytimes.com/2008/01/21/opinion/21iht-edwasserstrom.1.9374990.html (accessed 16 May 2014).

Whyte, M. K. 2010. *Myth of the social volcano: Perceptions of inequality and distributive injustice in contemporary China*. Stanford: Stanford University Press.

Whyte, Martin King. 1985. *Urban life in contemporary China*. Chicago: University of Chicago Press.

Wright, Erik Olin. 2005. *Approaches to class analysis*. Cambridge, UK: Cambridge University Press.

Wu, Jing. 2003. From 'long yang' and 'dui shi' to tongzhi: Homosexuality in China. *Journal of Gay & Lesbian Psychotherapy* 7 (1–2):117–43.

Wu, Xiaogang, and Zhuoni Zhang. 2015. The growth of Chinese professionals: A new middle class in the making. In *Handbook of Class and Social Stratification in China*. Cheltenham, UK: Edward Elgar. Available at http://works.bepress.com/xiaogang_wu/43/.

Yang, Huadong, Lili Tian, Jan Pieter Van Oudenhoven, Jacomijn Hofstra, and Qing Wang. 2010. Urban residents' subtle prejudice towards rural-to-urban migrants in China: The role of socioeconomic status and adaptation styles. *Journal of Community & Applied Social Psychology* 20 (3):202–16.

Yang, Li. 2012. Respect the villager's right to know. *China Daily*. Available online at http://usa.chinadaily.com.cn/opinion/2012-10/26/content_15850742.htm (accessed 19 February 2016).

You, Longbo, and Bing Xu. 2007. Gaige kaifang yilai woguo shehui jieceng jiegou bianqian de ruogantezheng. *Southeast Academic Research* 6: 116–21.

Bibliography

Zang, Xiaowei. 2008. Market transition, wealth, and status transitions. In *The New Rich in China: Future Rulers, Present Lives*. Goodman, David (ed). Oxon, UK: Routledge.

Zhang, Li. 2012. *In search of paradise: Middle-class living in a Chinese metropolis*. New York: Cornell University Press.

Zhang, Liming. 2005. Family Income over 60k–500k: Skepticism towards China's first middle class criteria. *Beijing Morning Post*. Available online at www.people.com.cn/GB/jingji/1037/3132404.html (accessed 29 July 2014).

Zhang, Yi. 2008. Political attitudes of the middle social stratum in today's China. *Social Sciences in China* (2):12.

Zhao, Suisheng. 2004a. *A nation-state by construction: Dynamics of modern Chinese nationalism*. Stanford: Stanford University Press.

Zhao, Suisheng. 2013. Foreign Policy Implications of Chinese Nationalism Revisited: The strident turn. *Journal of Contemporary China* 22 (82):535–53. doi: 10.1080/10670564.2013.766379.

Zhao, Yandong. 2004b. Chengshi renkou de jieceng rentong xianzhuang ji yingxiang yinsu. *Chinese Journal of Population Science* (5):19–25.

Zhen, Chen. 2001. Jieceng guishu yishi ji cehngyin fenxi. *Zhejiang Academic Research* (3):115–17.

Zhou, Xiaohong. 2008. Chinese middle class: Reality or illusion. In *Patterns of middle class consumption in India and China*. Jaffrelot, Christophe and Peter van der Veer (eds). 110–26.

Zhou, Yanqiu Rachel. 2006. Homosexuality, seropositivity, and family obligations: Perspectives of HIV-infected men who have sex with men in China. *Culture, Health & Sexuality* 8 (6):487–500.

Zhu, Guanglei. 1998. Studies of disintegration and recombination of social classes in modern China. *Teaching and Research* (5):19–28.

Index

Abrahamic religion 80
All Women Federation 101
America: Chinese attitude towards 92–93, 127; propagating universal values 81, 127; reacting to the rise of China 77; values *versus* Chinese values 80
Americanism 81
'American saboteurs' 71
angry youth 71
anti-Japanese movement 86–92, 126
anxiety of self-identified salaried class 20–21, 121
AQSIQ (Food Quality Safety Market Access System) 61
avant-garde democratic ideas 58–59

bao 'fa 'hu 25
Beijing 78
belonging, sense of 13, 24–25
block grants in health care sectors 35
Bourdieu, Pierre 16
boycotting Japanese goods 91–92, 126
British middle class 132–3

cadre *versus* professional dualism 8
calculability, social practice of 23
50-cent army 71
centralised technocracy 50
chan (property) 15
chenfen (social role) 14
children: being established as Chinese 115; education impacted by parents' socioeconomic status 43, 112–17, 118; studying abroad 114–15, 118; supplementary education for 114, 118
China: America's reaction to its rise 77; attitude towards America 92–93, 127; attitude towards India 94, 127; attitude towards Japan 86–92, 99, 126; attitude towards North Korea 94–96, 127; attitude towards Philippines 9, 96–97, 127; and Diaoyu (Senkaku) Island conflict 87, 89–91, 96, 126; diplomatic efforts of 91; foreign policy 77, 86–97, 126; how is perceived by other countries 77; military strength 90; and South China Sea territorial dispute 96–97
China Dream 8, 98
Chinese Communist Party (CCP) 77; membership 12, 57, 66, 122
Chinese exceptionalism 78–79
Chinese Ministry of Education 103
Chinese values: attitude towards 78–79; traditional 78–79, 82–86, 91, 98, 122–3; *versus* universal values 79–82, 98, 122–3
Chunling, Li 13, 33
chushen (social origin) 14
civic association 64
civic awareness 64
civil servants 33, 40, 44, 54–56, 59, 73
class *see also* specific types i.e. working class: categorisation mismatch with class identity 13; economic indicators of 13; elements of 14–15; experience mismatched with class position 13; intra-class cohesion 30; as mode of differentiation 8, 12; related to education 112–17; structure 7; subjective interpretation of terminologies 14–15; symbolic boundaries of 16
class agency 7
class conflict 56
class consciousness 71, 132
class habitus 16, 22, 25, 120, 121
class identity 99, 128–9; and class position discrepancy 4–5, 13, 15–17, 29, 121; mismatched with class position 13

146 *Index*

class markers 16; real estate holdings as 20–21
class position: and class identity discrepancy 4–5, 13, 15–17, 29; mismatched with class experience 13
Cobbett, William 69
collective balanced with the individual 6, 14, 41, 70, 81, 101, 107, 117–18, 124, 128
Communist Party *see* Chinese Communist Party (CCP)
compromise 6
conflict 56
Confucian ideology 3, 9, 24–26, 28, 31, 49, 75, 77, 124, 130
Confucianism 80, 81, 84, 122
Confucian merchants 9, 56
Confucian social order 122, 124–5, 130
consumerism threatening Chinese culture 1, 78, 84
consumption 8; as a conscious choice for the middle class 22–24; of luxury products 1
cultural and behavioural indicators of class 16, 18, 21–26, 28–29, 121
cultural break in history 83
cultural capital 113
Cultural Revolution 83, 95
cultural superiority 27–29, 78–79, 126
culture: being threatened by consumerism 78; of Japan highly regarded by Chinese 88, 126

democracy 77, 81; advocacy for 5, 50, 127; attitudes toward concepts of 57–59; different meanings of 2
developing countries and feelings towards them 86–97, 125–7
Diaoyu (Senkaku) Islands conflict 87, 89–91, 96, 126
dining out as class indicator 22–23
disaster relief effort 80, 93
downward identification tendency of middle-middle classes 20
'dragon slayers' 77
dual-accessibility system for health care 36–37

economic indicators for class identity 13, 15, 16, 21–22, 121
economic reforms *see* reform
economic security and the imagined middle class 26–29
economic well-being related to affording safe food 60

education: as characteristic of middle class 24, 40–43; as divider between migrant workers and middle class 109, 118; institution of 41; lack of access to 42; privatisation of 42–43; related to social class 112–17; unequal resource distribution between urban and rural 42; utilitarianism in 116; value of 41
elders, respect for 79
Engel's Coefficient 26
equality *versus* equity debate 55, 73
equity *versus* equality debate 55, 73
exogenous conception of the 'other' 24–25, 86–97, 125–7
expansionism 80
external individualistic factors 12

fairness: impacting democratic attitudes 58; and state responsibility for food safety 60
family background 12
fear in participating in sociopolitical events 66–67
filial piety 79, 82
five constant virtues 82
food safety concerns 59–63
foreign countries, attitude towards 86–97, 125–7
foreign influence and whether to allow or reject 78, 81–82
foreign policy of China 77, 86–97, 126
freedoms, individual and the state 5, 46–48, 50, 74, 83–84, 123, 132

Gates, Bill 27
gay by birth 105, 118
gay by choice 105, 118
geimenschaft community 83, 129
gender as a marginalised social group 101–4, 117
gesellschaft society 83, 129
Gidden's structuration theory 7
gongren jieji (class of workers) 14
gongxin jieceng (stratum of working salaries) 14, 15, 17; *see also* salaried class
government: being responsible for food safety 60–62; leading reforms 5, 59, 62–63, 64, 70, 74–75; limits of 5, 51, 63, 75, 124; reliance on 57–58, 122
grassroots civil society movements 57
grey income 33
guanxi 39, 85, 131; as causal factor in social inequity 52–54

Index

health care: dissatisfaction with 35–40; lack of transparency in spending 38–39
hedonism 81
homosexuality: as a marginalised group 104–7, 117–18, 128; viewed as a mental illness 104
homosexuals: adopting and raising children 106–7, 117; marriage of 106, 117
hospitals: dual-accessiblity system 36–37; and mixed ownership 36–38, 48
household registration system 8, 42; *see also hukou* 42, 73, 108–9
housing market and preoccupation with 20–21
Huang, Ray 118
hukou 42, 73, 108–9; *see also* household registration system 8, 42
human capital and increased social status 27
human rights 81
Hurricane Katrina 80, 93

ideological persistence 12
imagined middle class 13–14, 26–29
imperialism of America 93
income: determining the Chinese middle class 131; disparity 51–52; grey 33; result of income and not income amount determining class 19–20, 120–1; type indicating class identity 15, 17
India: Chinese attitude towards 94, 127; viewed as a backward country 94
individual: balance between state and 74; balanced with the collective 6, 14, 41, 70, 81, 101, 107, 117–18, 124, 128
individualism 79, 81; increase in 7, 8; rise of 83
individualistic heroism 81
inequity and regional differences 55–56
inflated income on paper 18
intermediate class of intellectuals 14
Internet 84
intolerance in society 84

Japan: animosity towards by China 86–92, 99, 126; culture highly regarded by Chinese 88, 126; national unity 88
jieji (class) 14
Jobs, Steve 27

Kim Jong Un 95
Kleinman, Arthur 129

land holdings not seen as respectable 28
lao baixing 70
law and order being maintained 46
leftover women 101–4, 117
literati 83

marginalised social groups 101–19, 127–9; homosexuals 104–7, 117–18, 128; migrant workers 107–12, 118, 127–8; women 101–4, 117
marital status 12
market 8, 75, 123, 131; *see also* privatisation; and role of the state 31–49
market reforms 35–36
media influence on people's opinion of America 93
medical savings accounts 35
Menicus' idea of people-based governance 75, 84, 124
men rejecting independent women 103–4
middlebrow 56, 80, 81, 83, 91
middle class 3, 4–5, 15, 128–31; attitudes towards welfare 32; awakening 69; British 132–3; Chinese national identity of 78–79, 97–100; choosing where to dine out 22–23; consumption as a conscious choice 22–24; cultural and behavioural aspects of 16, 18, 21–26, 28–29; cultural superiority 27–29, 78–79, 126; defined by exclusion 13–14, 25, 29, 120; as differentiated from salaried class 28–29, 121; heterogeneity of 2, 12; high civic awareness but low civic association 64; imagined economic security 26–29; interest in studying 8–9; liberal in Beijing 78; in middle of food chain 125; multiplicity of 2, 12; nationalism 77–100, 125–7; objective criteria for 10, 131; portrayed in Western media 131–2; rise of in developing countries 8; rising global nature of 78–79; self-identified 1–2, 9, 13, 15–16, 21–26, 131–2; and social stability 67–72; subjective sense of belonging 13, 24–25; subjectivity of identity 4–5, 15–17, 19–20, 29–30; summary of findings 120–34; survey respondents 9–11; viewing the state 31–49; as watchful observers 72, 76, 125, 133; Yin and Yang of 6, 117–19, 130–1
migrant workers 69; as a marginalised group 107–12, 118, 127–8; unequal treatment of 108–11
migration from rural to urban 107–9

148 *Index*

mixed ownership of hospitals 36–38, 48
monetarism 85
monotheism 80
moral decay 82, 84–85; causing food safety issues 61–62
morality 82–83, 98, 105
mortgage as burden 20
multi-candidate elections 57–58
multi-party elections 57

national humiliation 77, 126
nationalism 5, 77–100; popular 77, 98; pragmatic 81–82; state 77, 98
nepotism 53, 85
Ningbo 6, 9–11, 14–15, 18, 34, 36, 43, 55–56, 59, 63–65, 68, 78, 89, 95, 108, 110
normalised index 135
North Korea: Chinese attitude towards 94–96, 127; indoctrination of people 95

occupation as part of middle class identity 22
offline participation in sociopolitical events 64
online participation in sociopolitical events 64
other and exogenous conception of 24–25, 86–97, 125–7

panda huggers 77
paraxylene 63
parents' involvement in children's education 113–15
parvenu 25, 28, 121; *see also bao'fa'hu* 25
passive acceptance of sociopolitical events 66–67, 70, 76
past, romanticising of 85–86, 98
paternalistic state 31, 73–76, 122, 123
peer pressure causing food safety issues 62
pension and dissatisfaction with 43–45, 49
people-based governance 75, 80, 124
personal income tax as viewed by the middle class 32–35, 120–1
Philippines and Chinese attitude towards 96–97, 99, 127
political attitudes: conservative 76, 122; liberal 57–59
political freedom 5, 50
political liberty 57, 73, 123
political participation 63–70, 73, 76, 122; radical and violent viewpoint 72
poor: and education 43; and food safety 60; and medical care 37, 40; and social benefits 48

popular nationalism 77, 98
power as causal factor in social inequity 52
pragmatic nationalism 81–82
pragmatism 6, 72, 81–82, 117, 127–8
private sector, opening of 31
privatisation 5, 48–49, 123; *see also* market; in health care 35–40; in public services 31–32, 48–49
profit-driven moral decay causing food safety issues 61–62
property ownership and unfairness in 51–52
public attitudes and private behaivour discrepancy 4–6
public services being privatised 31–32, 48–49, 123

Rawls, John 51
reform: to be led by the government 5, 59, 62–63, 64, 70, 74–75; economic 84–85; pragmatism towards 72
relative deprivation 12, 18–21, 34–35, 73
respect for elders 79
rights consciousness 50, 124
rule by virtue 62
rural: and inequity 55–56; to urban migration 107–8

salaried class 1, 4–5, 13, 15–18; anxieties of 20–21, 34–35, 121; being unfairly taxed 33–34; as differentiated from middle class 28–29, 121; and dining out 22–23
salary *see* income
salaryman 14, 18
savings rate 44–45
segregation of school children 111–12
self balanced with the other 16, 24–25, 86–97, 117, 129–30
self-identified middle class 15–16, 21–26
Self-Strengthening Movement 89
significant correlation determination 135–6
significant factors determination 135
Sino-Japanese relations 86–92, 126
Sino-Japanese War 87
Sinology 85
social capital exchange 53–54
social class *see* class; middle class; specific classes
social conflict 60
social gentleman's agreement 75, 124
social identity: defining 128–9, 132–3; internalisation of 16–17, 18
social inequality 51–52, 55
social inequity 51–55

Index 149

social injustice 5, 73; being observatory rather than experienced 33
social issues 5–6
socialist state legacy 38, 52, 74–75, 124–5
social justice 51–57, 123
social reality 132
social representation 132
social reproduction theory 54
social stability: being maintained by the state 46–47; and middle class 67–72
social stabilizer 27–28
social status achieved through moral means 27–28
social stratification 8, 120
society: acceptance of homosexuals 105–6, 117–18; unfairness in 51–56
socioeconomic status impacting children's education 43, 112–17, 118
sociopolitical events 50–78; participation in 63–70, 73, 76, 122, 123–5
soft skills 53–54
South China Sea territorial disputes and Chinese attitude towards 96–97
stability and the middle class 67–72
standard deviations 135–6
standards of living and subjective assessment of 19
state: balance between individual and 74; being challenged 1–2; and individual freedoms 5, 46–48, 123; management of health care 36–38; perceived role of 45–48; reliance on 57–58, 122; and role in welfare 84; and role with the market 48–49, 123; supporters of 50; taking macroeconomic interventions 46; viewed by the middle class 31–49
state employment status 57
state nationalism 77, 98
state ownership 5
state sector employees 56
status quo: being challenged 2; maintaining 54, 69, 73, 76
stereotypes: of gender relations 103–4, 117; of non-superpowers 28, 94–97, 127
structure interwined with agency 7
subjective class identities 4–5, 15–17, 19–20, 29–30, 121
surveillance 48
suzhi 16, 17, 18, 24, 27, 28, 62, 121, 130, 133
symbolic factors for class identity 16, 24–25

Taoism 80, 81, 122, 130
tax evasion 33

tax inequality 34–35
Thompson, E. P. 9, 121
tradition: and preservation of 78–79, 82–86, 98, 122–3; revival of 85–86
traditional Chinese values 78–79, 82–86, 91, 98, 122–3

unequal treatment of migrant workers 108–11
unfair competition causing food safety issues 62
unfairness 51–56, 73
universal values: being propagated by America 81, 127; *versus* Chinese values 79–82, 98, 122–3
urban region: and inequity 55–56; rural migration to 107–8
utilitarianism 85

values, traditional Chinese 78–79, 82–86, 91, 98, 121, 122–3
violent expansionism 80
virtues, five constant 82

Wahrman, Dror 132, 133
war possibility between Japan and China 89–91
Weiming, Tu 31
welfare: attitudes of the middle class 32; government's reduced role in 31, 84
Wenchuan earthquake of 2008 80, 93
Westernisation of China 83
Western values *versus* Chinese values 79–82, 122–3
white collar workers 14
Whyte, Martin King 51, 55, 73
women: being marginalised 101–4, 117; leftover 101–4, 117; and work-family balance 102
work as part of salaried class identity 22
workers and peasants' social class 14
work-family balance for women 102
working class 13, 14; decline of culture 7

xenophobic 78, 94, 96, 98
Xiaohong, Zhou 13
xiaokang society 13, 133
Xiaotong, Fei 129

Yin and Yang of the middle class 6, 117–19, 130–1

Zemin, Jiang 62
Zhenhai PX incident 63–67

Taylor & Francis eBooks

Helping you to choose the right eBooks for your Library

Add Routledge titles to your library's digital collection today. Taylor and Francis ebooks contains over 50,000 titles in the Humanities, Social Sciences, Behavioural Sciences, Built Environment and Law.

Choose from a range of subject packages or create your own!

Benefits for you
- Free MARC records
- COUNTER-compliant usage statistics
- Flexible purchase and pricing options
- All titles DRM-free.

Benefits for your user
- Off-site, anytime access via Athens or referring URL
- Print or copy pages or chapters
- Full content search
- Bookmark, highlight and annotate text
- Access to thousands of pages of quality research at the click of a button.

REQUEST YOUR FREE INSTITUTIONAL TRIAL TODAY

Free Trials Available
We offer free trials to qualifying academic, corporate and government customers.

eCollections – Choose from over 30 subject eCollections, including:

Archaeology	Language Learning
Architecture	Law
Asian Studies	Literature
Business & Management	Media & Communication
Classical Studies	Middle East Studies
Construction	Music
Creative & Media Arts	Philosophy
Criminology & Criminal Justice	Planning
Economics	Politics
Education	Psychology & Mental Health
Energy	Religion
Engineering	Security
English Language & Linguistics	Social Work
Environment & Sustainability	Sociology
Geography	Sport
Health Studies	Theatre & Performance
History	Tourism, Hospitality & Events

For more information, pricing enquiries or to order a free trial, please contact your local sales team:
www.tandfebooks.com/page/sales

Routledge Taylor & Francis Group | The home of Routledge books

www.tandfebooks.com